Karen Morley

Lead like a coach

MACMILLAN

First published in 2023 by Major Street Publishing Pty Ltd

First published in India 2023 by Macmillan
an imprint of Pan Macmillan Publishing India Private Limited
707 Kailash Building
26 K. G. Marg, New Delhi 110001
www.panmacmillan.co.in

Pan Macmillan, The Smithson, 6 Briset Street, Farringdon, London EC1M 5NR
Associated companies throughout the world
www.panmacmillan.com

ISBN 978-93-95624-96-1

1 3 5 7 9 8 6 4 2

Internal design by Production Works
Printed in India by Gopsons Papers Pvt. Ltd., Noida

Praise for Dr Karen Morley and *Lead Like a Coach*

A delightful guide, full of important practical strategies for those of us who want to make a positive impact on stakeholders, our families and our communities. Karen Morley has written a must-read book for anyone considering doubling their engagement score! Read this book – and learn from one of the best.

Jovaline Lee, Senior Manager – Talent and Capability, Guild Group Insurance

Lead like a Coach, simply but powerfully articulates how to adapt one's leadership style to build more connected and engaged teams. By taking a coaching approach to leading teams, not only will your direct report relationships and effectiveness improve but your teams will learn and promote these behaviours, creating a wider culture of performance. Dr Morley uses real case studies to support her work and provides tools that will prove invaluable to any leadership role.

Duncan Phillips, Chief Operating Officer, TerryWhite Chemmart

I first met Karen Morley at a time I was having difficulty with a number of work interactions... For the first time I learnt to see how my beliefs, vulnerabilities and successes impacted how I responded to others within the work environment. Karen lifted me out of the details of the situation and helped me observe myself. I finally appreciated that your work success is not just about the technical skills and delivery but is truly influenced by connectivity and how each person creates the connections. My 'light-bulb' moment was transformative and I believe was fundamental to my growth as a leader. It is an insight I try to pass on to others. I cannot think of anyone more skilled to impart the knowledge within this book and am so pleased Karen has chosen to widely share her guidance.

Dr Charmaine Gittleson, Chief Medical Officer, CSL Behring

Having been lucky enough to benefit from executive coaching from Karen a few years ago, I was very keen to read *Lead like a Coach*. As always, Karen coaches you through the steps with great insight and real case studies. All you have to do is to trust in her and commit to making the changes – the benefits will always follow! I hope you enjoy and get as much out of this book as I did.

Paul Axup, Group Financial Controller, Aurecon

The intuitive, practical and relevant case studies provided in *Lead like a Coach* encourage and enthuse all to be coaches as required.

Paul Menzies, Chair – Advisory Board, SimPPLY

This book is a must-read for any leader. I had the pleasure of having Karen as a coach and she taught me the importance of coaching in building and leading an effective team. Karen helped me to use coaching as a way to build trust in the team. I realised that the more I used a coaching approach, my team also started to coach each other. We started engaging and communicating a lot more effectively as a team.

Lucy Zhou, Corporate Finance Manager, Jardines

Lead Like a Coach offers powerful practical advice, based on compelling evidence, on how to lift your game for the benefit of the people you lead. Of particular interest was the section on 'asking Coaching questions' requiring your team members to find solutions rather than being directed.

Irrespective of where you are in your career or how well you currently manage your team, Karen Morley offers all leaders an opportunity to revisit or hone their coaching skills for the mutual benefit of all parties. The content of Karen's book so impressed me that I have ordered copies for every leader of people in my division.

Phil Turnbull, Executive General Manager, RACV

While it's one thing to lead, or be called 'a leader', the reality is today's business world demands much more. There is a genuine art to developing the skills to become an effective coach and through this unlock your own potential as a true leader.

Lead Like a Coach is a well written and considered book that brings to life practical insights and examples of how even an experienced leader can better connect, engage and bring teams on the journey to unlock their true potential.

Michael Schneider, Managing Director – Bunnings

Lead like a Coach is a clear, engaging roadmap designed to help leaders let go of the traditional command control structures and really focus on how to be a better leader by connecting with and coaching our teams. I've been the beneficiary of Karen's coaching over the past couple of years and am very excited to see that her tools and approaches translate so well into book form, meaning her wisdom can now reach and benefit a much broader audience.

Emily Phillips, Manager – Regional Services, Melbourne Water

What an honour to be given a 'sneak peek' into this little gem of a book! Once I started to read it, I realised that this was so practical, easy to read, and filled with anecdotes about others at various stages of their leadership journey, I found the pages almost turned themselves! I loved that I did not need to read it from cover to cover – instead, I discovered a helpful range of activities and tools which can be employed in any order – reflecting Karen's deep understanding that leaders are busy people, and one or two new 'tricks' at a time is sometimes all we can manage.

Lisa Evans, Executive General Manager, Corporate Services, Melbourne Airport

Lead Like a Coach is a must-read for all leaders who are committed to ensuring their direct reports, both individually and as a team, reach their full potential. If you use the practical coaching advice, tools and techniques included in Karen's book you will be much better able to inspire, empower and energise them, which will lead to more sustainable and higher organisational performance. You will also leave a much greater legacy.

Nicholas S. Barnett, Chief Executive Officer, Insync

My career would not be where it is today without the candid, thought-provoking and 'call-to-action' coaching from Karen over many years. She taught me how to navigate my journey – through the highs and lows – with an honesty that enabled me to challenge conventions and take ownership of my destiny. This book is a must-read – it gives us the methodology, tools and encouragement to ignite the coaching pathway for all. We owe this to our teams, and to ourselves to always strive to be better leaders.

Karen Gardner, Senior Director, Head R&D Quality Assurance, Global Quality, Seqirus

In *Lead Like a Coach*, Dr Karen Morley shares with us the wealth of her knowledge gained from years of hands-on experience coaching leaders, as well as rigorous academic study in the field. Her material is presented in a practical and meaningful manner, thoughtfully referencing relevant workplace studies and utilising specific case studies to tangibly illustrate her advice. She poses questions to the reader throughout, allowing them to reflect on their own situations and directly apply the learnings. This is a valuable addition to the toolbox for every leader, seasoned and aspiring.

Dr Emma Ball, Director, Therapeutic Area Strategy & Business Development, CSL Limited

Today, as organisations strive to provide 'more with less', discretionary effort from team members is becoming an increasingly important asset. Those organisations with leaders who can build high levels of trust within their respective teams, have a very real advantage in terms of both engagement and, as a consequence, performance. Drawing on Karen's wealth of experience in this area, *Lead Like a Coach* provides some very practical and easy-to-understand advice that all leaders, irrespective of their existing approach, will find very useful in bringing out the best in a team.

Michael Howard, Chief Financial Officer, Officeworks

I am so grateful to Karen Morley for writing this book. *Lead Like a Coach* is an invaluable guide for all leaders – current, soon-to-be and ever-learning – seeking better understanding of themselves and those they work with. In this book, Karen draws on her extensive background as a scholar, teacher and mentor to guide us clearly through the why, how and when of coaching. It's packed full of great insights and case studies from real leaders dealing with real issues; after reading *Lead Like a Coach*, I've come away feeling more confident in my leadership style and abilities. As Karen says upfront, learning to lead like a coach can help lift the weight off your shoulders, so grab a copy of this book, put on your 'coaching cap' and trust in yourself and others!'

A/Professor Erica Wilson, A/Deputy Vice Chancellor (Academic) Southern Cross University

About the author

Dr Karen Morley helps leaders to realise their full potential. She helps leaders to meet the challenges of growing engaged, motivated, productive people who love their work, respect their bosses and are proud of their organisations.

Karen appreciates that the work of leadership is challenging. Her career has been devoted to working with leaders to influence their development. She continues to admire those exceptional leaders whom everyone loves to work with and who get great results. Her goal is to help spread a bit of this magic to all leaders. We need to lighten the weight of leadership and make it more enjoyable and fulfilling.

Karen is an experienced executive coach and greatly enjoys coaching individual leaders. She has coached leaders at organisations as diverse as the Australian Institute of Company Directors (AICD), Allens, BHP Billiton, Broadspectrum, CBA, Coles, CSL, CUB, Downer, ExxonMobil, GCC, KPMG, Latitude Financial, Lendlease, L'Oreal, Lumleys, Medibank, Melbourne Airport, Melbourne Water, Monash Health, Officeworks, Orica, QBE, RACV, Rural Finance, Target, UGL, University of Melbourne and VisionStream.

Karen brings broad experiences, top professional credentials and a variety of perspectives. She's a registered psychologist with a desire to align what leaders do with the available evidence for what works. Besides being an executive coach and leadership developer, Karen has held executive roles in government and higher education, and her approach is informed by her experience in these roles. Along the way, she completed a doctorate in leadership, published *Gender Balanced Leadership: An Executive Guide* and has written numerous other working and white papers. She is an Honorary Fellow of the University of Melbourne and a Director at ANZSOG.

Karen lives in Melbourne. She Chairs the board of Emerge Women and Children's Support Network which assists women and children affected by domestic violence.

Working with Karen Morley

Karen works with executives and human resource leaders from a range of different organisations to help their leaders fulfil their potential, to make leadership more inclusive and collaborative and to help grow the coaching capability of their leaders.

If you are interested in finding out how Karen might be able to work with you or your organisation, please visit www.karenmorley.com.au, email kmorley@karenmorley.com.au or call +61 438 215 391.

Contents

Introduction

The best leaders are also coaches

Everyone these days seems to need to get more done. The pace of life has increased, and we have much higher expectations of what we should do with our time.

After school, my step-grandson attends Auskick, reading lessons and a raft of different activities. His party calendar is pretty full too. We sometimes need to book three weeks in advance to spend a weekend afternoon with him. And he's only five and a half years old!

Expectations on leaders are increasing. Leaders are expected to get more done. They are expected to be available 24/7, to respond as if all information is always at their fingertips and to work across multiple time zones.

In our 21st century world of abundance, paradoxically we seem to have fewer resources. We are captured by everyday pressures to do more, be more, know more... not to mention be more resilient and happier!

The challenges magnify further. Not only is it important to do more and be more, leaders need to help their team members to do the same. And that is no mean feat.

Many leaders I meet and coach feel these pressures like a weight on their shoulders. It's hard to be inspiring when you're weighed down by a heavy load.

The core proposition of this book is that leading like a coach will help you to lighten the burden you feel and give you more energy. By refocusing the way you engage with your team members you can double their engagement and get more and better work done.

This book is for leaders who:

- care about the people they lead;
- care about their own success; and
- want to make a positive impact on their stakeholders, their families and their communities.

Many leaders are still hesitant about coaching. They are not confident in their coaching ability.

Occasionally a leader will confide in me that coaching feels risky. It feels as if you are giving up control. When you feel that you are under huge workload pressures, giving up control seems like the last thing you should do.

Underneath it all, there's a common fear that if your team does all the work – working at their maximum capability – what will *you* be doing? What will be your value? You are good at doing the work, you were promoted because you are, and now you have to stop doing the work. Hmmm, so what *do* you do?

You coach, of course!

Why you need to develop a coaching culture

The next challenge is that while many organisations say they want a coaching culture, they don't make it easy for leaders to coach. Many organisations operate as if early 20th-century

Taylorism[1] worked. In the 21st century world of complexity and change, a style based on control is only going to be occasionally effective. It is necessary to let go of last century's leadership habits.

Taylor's early 20th century theory saw human systems as machine-like, and so control was the appropriate approach to exercising authority. Then we saw humans as rational actors: the job of the boss was to create order. As the 20th century closed we began to understand human systems as complex and adaptive, so the role of authority needed to shift. The new focus was on interpreting the complexity, making sense of it for others.

As we begin to see human systems as more open and flexible, ways to *manage* the system become less relevant. In open, flexible systems, the approach to authority shifts to one of *leading*. Authority no longer fits the person into the system, but enables the person to navigate the system themselves. Figure 1 presents this development.

Figure 1 – How management has been replaced by leadership

Century	Human systems are	Approach to authority	
21st	Open	Orient/catalyst	Lead
Late 20th	Complex	Interpret	Manage
Mid 20th	Rational	Order	
Early 20th	Machine-like	Control	

This is where the value of coaching becomes obvious. For a person to successfully navigate an open system they must be able to create and use their own power, to be granted the freedom to grow and exercise their own authority and to be authorised to realise their full potential.

If you adopt a coaching style in your leadership, and support and develop your team, they will most likely do this. They will feel more inspired, committed and satisfied. As coaching becomes more 'natural', 'drops in' and becomes engrained in your leadership, your team will become more engaged.

Coaching will become as empowering and energising for you as it is for your team.

As you increase your coaching, trust your team more and delegate more, you will gain a greater sense of purpose in your leadership. You will lead in a more congruent and human way, and relieve yourself of some of the pressures of the responsibility that comes with many management roles. The weight will lift from your shoulders. You will be uplifted.

My goal with this book is to help you to be an exceptional leader. To be a leader everyone wants to work with, who brings out the best in others, and who gets great results – and that means being a great coach.

+ Get out of the play and into the coaching box

Martin draws many parallels between his experience coaching his team at work with his experience coaching his son's under-12 soccer team. One of the key lessons he has learned is about the field from which the leader chooses to engage.

During practice, the previous soccer coach and some of the parents usually took up positions on the field and joined the play. This was justified as a way to model tactics to the younger players, but largely, in Martin's view, it continued because the parents had fun playing.

Martin changed this pretty quickly. He agreed that it was fun as a coach to get onto the field and play with the team. However, he saw too many downsides. The players had fewer opportunities to learn through trial and error. They had less opportunity to learn from their own mistakes and to think for themselves. He felt that if he was on the sideline, and the players didn't understand or know how to do something, he could always stop the play and model that for them.

Playing as a team at practice gave the team greater autonomy on the field on game day. Once the whistle blew, the players had to work out their tactics on their own. This was better preparation; it gave them more direct experience to use in their games.

When the more competent adult players took to the field they were unwittingly reducing the learning that the players could do. For Martin, these were some of the same principles that guided his leadership at work. With his work teams, he placed a great deal of emphasis on allowing them space for trial and error. He thought that it might be important to model and to join in with the work for team members who were just starting out. Mostly, the approach he relied on to get his team to perform well and continue to develop was to use his coaching tactics with them. He gave team members the opportunity to talk issues through and patiently encouraged them to identify what they would do.

He wanted to raise their confidence so that they would take away their ideas and try them out.

Martin's advice is for managers to get out of the play and into the coaching box. When you play in the game you can't see the whole, you're serving your own needs and you're interfering with the learning of your team. From the coaching box, you have a clearer line of sight on what's going on in the game. You can see who's doing well, who needs help, where the gaps are, and what tactics you need to use to get the next part of the work done.

Now, you won't find too many sporting analogies in this book. There are some, but it's the style of interaction, not the field of interaction, that counts as coaching for me. Some sporting coaches are great coaches. Others aren't. Some organisational leaders are great coaches. Others aren't. *Lead Like a Coach* focuses on developing a coaching style to use in situations where there is a team of (two or more) people who need to accomplish something together.

Why I wrote this book

I've devoted my career to helping leaders develop. Having coached hundreds of leaders over thousands of hours, I am amazed at how much growth is possible when people are willing to be coached. I've written this book to spread the magic of coaching to all leaders. We need to lighten the weight of leadership and make it more enjoyable and fulfilling. I hope that this book does that for you.

With this book, I give you my coaching resources to help you coach yourself to become a better coach. I encourage you to do the assessments at the end of Part I to identify the coaching capabilities you are good at, and those you'd like to develop.

Part II provides information on how to develop your coaching capabilities, no matter where you are starting from. You can read the chapters in sequence, but you don't *need* to. Having identified your development goals, head to the relevant chapter to find out more.

You will find activities in each part that provide specific guidance on what to do and how to review your progress as coach. Use the activities to coach yourself to being a better coach.

There's plenty to work with here; if you'd like more resources, go to my website https://karenmorley.com.au/leadlikeacoach.

PART I

Why you should coach

1

Organisations are better places when leaders coach

Coaching, not controlling, is a compelling way for leaders to improve team performance. Leaders who coach create and grow trust. When trust is high, people are engaged and energised. They work harder, for longer and are more productive.

Leaders who coach double their engagement scores

In *Declining Global Productivity Growth: The Fix*, Jim Clifton wrote: *"What if... we doubled the number of engaged workers...? It begins by changing what leaders believe. And then changing how they lead."*[2]

Leaders are under great pressure to produce results at a faster pace, using fewer resources and where there are many more options to choose from. Unfortunately, most leaders react to this by adopting a command-and-control style of leadership. The pressure takes them over. They don't delegate enough, they become overworked themselves and end up feeling overburdened. Teams disengage from leaders who control. Rather than increasing their performance, their work output falls and they become discouraged. Efforts by command-and-control leaders to produce more become counterproductive. Instead, they and their teams produce less, and increase the risk of burn-out.

Leaders who coach approach their responsibilities very differently. They focus on the team and how the team can be supported to produce better results. Rather than command and control, they develop and support.

Leaders who coach grow trust

Trust is cultivated when leaders take the time to show interest in supporting and developing others. Delegation is a good proxy for trust. When leaders readily delegate work and responsibility to their team members they show them that they trust them.

Letting go of control

Amy was invited to accept a senior leadership role for which she had no technical training. She took up the challenge, but she had doubts about her fit for the role – and so did her team members. They worked in a security function, and for many years they hadn't seen much change in how they operated. The former manager had been a technical expert who had spent all of his career in security. Amy's team members were all technical security experts.

About two years into the role, Amy was continuing to question whether this was a good fit for her. She felt that she needed to be tougher and more controlling and assert herself as the leader. She had a fairly blunt and direct style anyway, and she felt she needed to keep it ramped up.

While this behaviour seemed to be expected, the feedback was that she overdid it, and this was very frustrating.

Then, a critical incident occurred. A large theft occurred in one of the regional teams. Amy worked with her Regional Manager and their team to deal with this. They followed the process and executed the response plan. But the HR team stepped in to challenge the way a particular staff member was dealt with. Rather than approaching the Regional Manager, HR came directly to Amy in Head Office.

Initially, Amy was ready to charge in to defend the actions of the Regional Manager as being 'the right thing to do'. From her point of view, things had gone very well. The theft situation had been well controlled. She wanted to make sure that her team's actions were properly understood and they didn't experience blowback. She had put on her armour to go into battle.

Luckily, we just happened to have a coaching session scheduled the morning prior to the showdown. The upshot of our coaching session was that Amy decided to reframe the intervention from HR. Rather than being something she needed to control, she saw it as an opportunity her team and HR could learn from. She saw that she needed to step out of the way for that to happen.

And she did. She told HR that she wouldn't be meeting with them, but that her Regional Manager and his team would be. She spoke with her Regional Manager, told him what was happening and why. She spoke with the Head of HR and asked that they to do the same.

What did Amy do differently?

Looking back at the case study, Amy learned a new way of dealing with a challenging situation. By letting go of control, and trusting her Regional Manager to manage the internal fallout, she did several things.

1. Amy tried on a coaching cap. She redefined her role from manager to expert and let her Regional Manager be the expert in a situation that had occurred in his patch. She set out to coach him in how to manage the situation.
2. By setting up a learning frame, she focused attention on the future, and what is possible, rather than on the past and what was done.
3. This enabled the focus of action to be on opportunities rather than mistakes.
4. She didn't use her power in a coercive way as she first intended, to prove that her way was the right way. By stepping back, she showed trust in her Regional Manager by delegating responsibility back where it belonged. She spoke to him about what she was doing and why she was doing it, and she offered him guidance and support. The discussion between the Regional Manager and HR was on how they could ensure that everyone's needs were met if such a situation occurred again.

Amy's mindset had shifted to be more open. It was more collaborative and generous, thinking: how can we make this work? This event had unexpected flow-on benefits. Shifting to a coaching mindset meant Amy didn't have to be the security expert. She felt more congruent in her role as a coach. She could spend her time being more strategic and innovative, rather than trying to learn a new functional skill – a skill that her team had in abundance. She trusted more, delegated more.

She told her team her story of how she had felt a lack of fit, why she was no longer going to try to fit, and why she valued their technical skills. Her relationship with her team members became deeper. She showed greater trust in the team (and herself) by delegating more to them. The team has repaid that by generating more ideas, making more suggestions and taking more leadership actions. Amy continues to take a coaching rather than a controlling stance, and this is spreading out to other stakeholders in the business.

She's living the differences between a commanding, directive culture and an empowering, coaching culture (see Figure 1.1 below). She's feeling more congruent, is growing relationships that are more positive, and giving herself space to sweat the big stuff.

Figure 1.1 – Command-and-control vs coaching leadership styles

	Commanding culture	Coaching culture
Roles	Manager as expert	Person as expert on self
Time	The past: what holds me back?	The future: what propels me forward?
Actions	Mistakes: what went wrong?	Opportunities: what do we need/want?
Power	Coercion: do it my way	Attraction: how will you do it?
Mindset	Show me how it will work	How can we make this work?

It's clear that coaching produces better results than a command-and-control leadership style. Yet the command-and-control style continues to be used. Why? Because coaching goes against the grain for many leaders. While 80% of organisations say they are keen to develop a coaching culture, a coaching style goes against the grain for many of them too[3]. They continue to reward command-and-control styles. A core proposition of command-and-control is that the people at the top make the decisions and others aren't to be trusted. This is just bad for business.

The key reasons that leaders like Amy don't coach more is they are:

- captured by everyday pressures to produce results;
- not confident in their coaching capability; and
- unclear or unaware of the connection between coaching, team engagement and productivity.

When trust is high, engagement is high and more work gets done

The connection between high team engagement and superior organisational performance is well known. Engaged teams show 24% to 59% less turnover in staff, 70% fewer safety incidents occur and there's 41% less absenteeism than in disengaged teams. Engaged teams enjoy 10% higher customer ratings and 21% greater profitability[4]. A 5% increase in engagement equals a 3-point increase in revenue growth in the following year[5].

Gallup global engagement meta-analysis shows that top quartile business units double the productivity of bottom quartile units. Those at the 99th percentile have four times the success of those at the bottom percentile[6].

Gallup's analytics show that less than a third of the workforce is engaged[7]. About one quarter (24%) in their research are actively disengaged[4]. Only 14% of Australian and New Zealand employees show up to work each day *"with enthusiasm and the motivation to be highly productive"*[8].

Most organisations could substantially improve performance through improved engagement.

Coach more and make your organisation a better place to be

Leaders can make the biggest difference to engagement. Leaders who coach enrol the disengaged and the doubtful. When leaders have the right coaching skills, and coach frequently, they generate engaged and empowered work teams (see Figure 1.2).

Figure 1.2 – How coaching leads to greater engagement and work effort

Coaching	Engagement	Work effort	
Very frequently	Empowered	4 x	Lead
Frequently	Engaged	2 x	
Occasionally	Enrolled	1	Manage
Rarely	Doubtful	½ x	
Never	Disengaged	¼ x	

Jim Clifton, in his popular Chairman's Blog, said "*Leaders are the biggest part of the problem with engagement. They are responsible for 70% of the variance in workplace culture.*"[9]

Bad bosses are the biggest single reason people leave organisations. Leaders carry the biggest responsibility for workplace culture and productivity[10]. The biggest challenge to productivity is that the practice of management hasn't changed in 30 years[9]. Management practices need to change for productivity to change.

Gallup's and other research also shows that great bosses are the biggest single reason people stay in organisations. According to the research, the team leader is the silver bullet for engagement and productivity[10]. Top team leaders contribute about 48% higher profitability to their companies than average managers[11]. They do that by creating a high development experience for their team.

If you do not already have good engagement with your teams, coaching can help you achieve it. And if engagement is already good, coaching will help you to get more work done.

If you coach more, you will create a workplace that everyone enjoys more.

Bad bosses are the biggest single reason people leave organisations... great bosses are the biggest single reason people stay in organisations.

Each section is this book has activities that help you translate the tips and tools into action. Below is the first. All the activities are designed to turn your reading into learning and your practice into competence. You might make it a goal to do all the activities, or just a few. It's your choice.

Activity

1. Review your team's engagement scores. How actively engaged are your team members?
2. What improvement would you like to see in the engagement of your team?

2

Coaching is contagious

Any time someone is coached well, they become more coach-like themselves. This is what I call the contagion effect. The contagion of coaching sets off a ripple effect. Why does this happen?

When you coach people in your organisation, they begin to find their own answers and become more resourceful. People work more effectively together because they engage in dialogue. They listen and ask questions rather than tell others what to do. They see resistance as an opportunity to explore other perspectives, rather than as a threat. The nature of conversations between people changes. Interactions become more positive. The coaching style ripples out as more people enjoy its experience.

The contagion effect of coaching means that the efforts of each leader are magnified through the efforts of everyone they coach.

Coaching to develop your team

Jackie, leader of the Marketing Group at Next Jump[12], received feedback that she was seen as putting herself first. It was preventing her from being offered leadership opportunities. She acknowledged that she put her own success ahead of the success of others. She was on a quest to get to the top. She couldn't see any other way to do it.

It took some getting used to, but once Jackie realised that her behaviour was limiting her aspirations, she worked out a plan for change. She started by coaching once a month, with the deliberate intention of helping others to be successful. That was a challenge, but she stuck with it. She started coaching more frequently – weekly, then daily.

After about a year, the feedback she received had changed remarkably. Others around her were developing, and she could see the benefits of her shift in leadership style spreading across the business.

She had thought that if she spent so much time coaching, she wouldn't be able to get her job done. If she spent her time on *others*, *she* wouldn't be successful.

But what Jackie has realised is that she can be successful in a completely different way. When leaders coach, they create a culture that is empowering and energising. When coached, people develop, their motivation elevates, and they engage more deeply. In Jackie's case, she was coached by her boss to become a better coach. She recognised how much she was developing by coaching others rather than trying to succeed on her own. Her team, and people across the organisation, were able to develop as she did.

When leaders coach, the benefits spread

Jackie's organisation in the case study above, Next Jump, makes it a priority that each person must be counted on to help others succeed. They deliberately embrace the coaching ripple effect.

By being deliberately developmental[12], a coaching culture empowers and develops current leaders. At the same time, it grows future leaders.

What is evident in Jackie's story is the shift from an individual to a collective benefit. She was a commanding, controlling boss. It took great effort for her to switch from being a controller to a coach. She stopped asking 'How can I be my best?' Instead she asked 'How can I help my team to be its best?'

Leaders who coach *ask*:

- 'How can I help my team to be its best?' rather than command;
- 'How do I help the teams I am a part of to best meet our challenges?' rather than compete; and
- 'How do I balance an investment in future capability with a focus on results right now?' rather than control.

Leaders who coach cultivate trust by supporting and developing others. They do what they can to equip others to do their best work. Not only does more work of a better quality get done, it has the enormous benefit of relieving the 'power stress'[13] that leaders feel. While Jackie continues to work on her coaching skills, the rewards of her new leadership style are tangible. She doesn't have to fear failure, as she previously did.

High trust extends oxytocin release, which increases wellbeing and happiness.

In a recent study, a high-trust workplace meant 74% less stress, 106% more energy at work, 13% fewer sick days and 40% less burnout.

In high-trust organisations, people:

- enjoy their jobs 60% more;
- are 70% better aligned with their company's purpose;
- feel 66% closer to their colleagues; and
- feel a 41% greater sense of accomplishment[14].

How you can spread the benefits of coaching further

Very frequent coaching establishes relationships where trust is complete. This substantially benefits work effort and output (see Figure 2.1 below).

Figure 2.1 – How coaching builds trust

Coaching	Trust is	Work effort	
Very frequently	Complete	4 x	Lead
Frequently	Coactive	2 x	Lead
Occasionally	Conditional	1	Manage
Rarely	Constrained	½ x	Manage
Never	Absent	¼ x	Manage

Jackie is lucky that she is working in an organisation that is uncompromisingly focused on development and coaching[12]. Despite the clear benefit of coaching to the measures that matter, most organisations continue to reward practices that fracture collective will. They:

- reinforce power differentials by rewarding command-and-control styles, where only top leaders make decisions;
- over-recognise individual and under-recognise collective effort; and
- develop senior leaders while neglecting the development of those on the frontline.

Whether or not your organisation supports coaching, you can still increase your own coaching capability. You can create your own coaching ripples by coaching your team. Find peers and colleagues across your organisation who share your interest in coaching and set up your own community of practice. By agreeing to coach each other on your coaching development, you can continue to inspire and motivate each other.

Example: Alex tells the story of a young female engineer who had observed her in a meeting. She approached Alex to say that she would like to have a conversation about how she leads. She asked Alex how she developed the confidence to speak about a particular topic in the meeting; what she felt and how she did it. Rather than answer directly, Alex asked coaching questions. What did you observe? How does that strike you? What would you have done? What did you feel was the challenge? For Alex, in every conversation she's being the coach.

How coaching realises potential

By focusing on the future, leaders give others the opportunity to imagine the future. Rather than being stale, set or safe, coaching opens up limitless possibilities to grow talents and skills to their full potential. Figure 2.2 highlights the distinctions between a future-oriented rather than a backward-looking focus, and between a controlling and a coaching approach.

Figure 2.2 – Future-oriented coaching vs backward-looking control

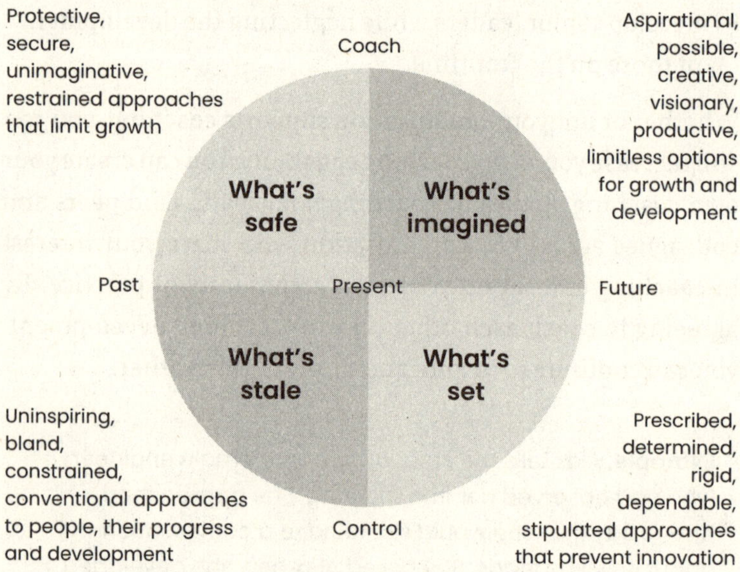

A controlling style that focuses on the past is stale and out of date. It constrains growth and holds back development. A controlling style that is future-focused helps to grow capabilities, but by being fixed on set responses – the tried and true – it limits innovation and autonomy.

A coaching approach that is based on the past is highly protective. It may feel safe, but with its protective cocoon-like wrapping, growth and innovation are suppressed.

A coaching approach that is future-oriented gives the person you are coaching the opportunity to generate their own options for growth. They can pursue what they can imagine. It offers the greatest promise to fulfil their potential.

When leaders practise future-oriented coaching they are opening the door to team members' aspirations, creating the opportunity for them to grow and develop to the greatest extent possible.

It's not just team members who benefit when leaders coach. Leaders also benefit when they coach.

Leaders feel powerful and energised when they coach. The action of coaching itself becomes rewarding. Rather than telling others what you already know, you hear others' interpretations and the decisions they make. By developing others, leaders are also developing themselves.

> **Example:** Lee was promoted from being a team leader to a manager of team leaders. As she coached them to lead their teams well, she realised that she was learning from their experiences and suggestions. Coaching was opening up new options for her too. It was a continuing prompt for how she should lead and improve herself.

Activity

1. How well do you balance your attention between future capability needs versus results right now?
2. What might you do to get the balance right?
3. What percentage of your time is focused on skills needed in the past rather than skills needed for the future?
4. Is your focus sufficiently aspirational and motivational for your team?

3

How much and how well do you coach now?

Having set the field of play for coaching, it's now time for try-outs. What is your coaching capability right now? How do you rate your coaching skills?

To help you assess your capability and to focus your development, I'll introduce you to three models I regularly use when I coach. They are:

1. **The why:** a framework to understand how adults develop
2. **The what:** a continuum to focus your development
3. **The how:** a scoreboard to help chart the course of your development as a coach.

You can apply these ideas to your own development as you work through this book. You can also use them as a guide when you coach others.

The why: a framework to understand how adults develop

Having greater insight into how adult learning occurs will maximise your own learning. You will be better able to support others as they learn.

How do you see your own development to date? What is your appetite for authority and the challenges of leading others?

Being responsible for a team that achieves results is very different to being an individual contributor. To be a good leader you need to be comfortable exercising authority. As you move into roles that are bigger and give you more responsibility, you need to adapt the way you see yourself – and you need to adapt the way you value the work you do.

Adult development and exercising authority are closely linked. Exercising authority effectively means being able to see things from many perspectives. Responsibility for resources and making decisions is easier if you see multiple ways of doing things. You don't have to give up your own position to do this. You can understand the views and opinions of others as you strengthen or clarify your own.

Coaching means taking multiple perspectives without necessarily advocating one over the other. It requires listening and patience. It requires the ability to separate you as 'subject' from you as 'object'. The ability to take an objective, detached perspective on how you enact your role, and how you engage with your team members, will help you to coach.

Jennifer Garvey Berger's[15] work on adult development, *Simple Habits for Complex Times: Powerful Practices for Leaders*, is helpful for assessing your relationship with authority and leadership. As Jennifer says, "*A growth stance opens us to new possibilities in ourselves – it leads others to become bigger in our company.*"

Rather than being 'had by' the demands of leadership roles, effective leaders hold awareness of but are not daunted by them. This requires the ability to stand back from what you do and critically reflect on your actions and the impact you make – all offer great benefit for the leader as coach.

There are four main forms of mind:

1. Self-sovereign
2. Socialised
3. Self-authored
4. Self-transforming (see Figure 3.1 below).

Figure 3.1 – The four forms of mind

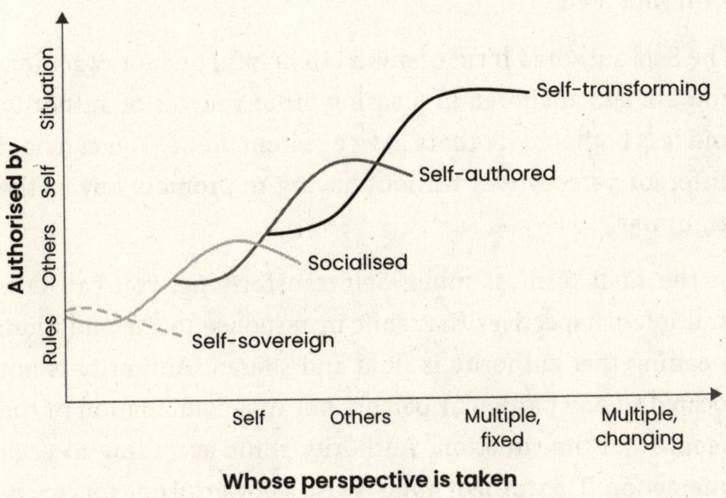

At any point in time you might be fully in one form, or moving between two forms. It's helpful to reflect on where you are at.

The Self-sovereign mind is just as it sounds. The only perspective that can be taken in this form is your own. Other perspectives are either not noticed or not understood. This is very recognisable in young children.

In the Socialised form of mind authority comes from others. The views of important others shape your own opinions of yourself. You look to others for the right answer, to judge what's right and wrong. When different views are expressed, you may feel internal conflict.

Early-to-mid career leaders are often moving from the Socialised to the Self-authored form of mind. In this form, authority is found in the self. When others disagree it might be unpleasant, but it doesn't cause internal confusion. From this perspective you can understand the views of others and compare them with your own.

The Self-authored form of mind is a helpful one for coaching. You are less anchored in pleasing other sources of authority, and less bothered if others have different views. You can hold different perspectives without having to promote any as the 'right way'.

In the final form of mind, Self-transforming, you can take multiple perspectives that shift in response to the situation, meaning that authority is fluid and shared. Authority is not located in any particular person, but in a combination of the people and the situation. Authority shifts according to each interaction. This form of mind is also a powerful one for coaching, as it allows you to think flexibly according to the context.

Questioning authority

When I met with Tom to begin our coaching program, he was struggling with his own sense of leadership identity. His coaching program began with this statement:

'I know my strengths. I'm very good at managing relationships and being collaborative and at strategic thinking. I know that I overplay my strengths, and that I keep relying on them to avoid the business/management stuff. I question deeply what authority is, and feel challenged by it.'

For Tom, authority was tightly bound with status, management and execution. His view of status, management and execution was very negative.

We agreed that a key goal of coaching would be to work out how to challenge his perspective that authority and warmth were contradictory.

Tom saw status, power and authority as intertwined. The bundling up of these concepts was creating a barrier in his thinking about his next possible career moves, and what fitted with his self-image. He was experiencing a dilemma. He thought he'd like a promotion – he was seen as promotable – but he couldn't see what role he would have that would sit comfortably with his self-image.

Tom labelled a prominent organisational leader as 'insincere'. This was someone who excelled on the execution side. Tom identified that this was part of his struggle with authority. What he realised he was doing was conflating execution, status and insincerity. He really didn't want to be like this person whose behaviour he viewed as distasteful.

Tom avoided directing his team to get things done because he valued having friendly relationships with his team. He thought that a drive to execution meant that he couldn't have friendly relationships with them. On reflection, he was able to articulate that what sat underneath this was his self-image as likeable. Likeability and authority didn't go together.

Being likeable was mixed up with being warm and having good emotional intelligence. Tom was praised for his self-awareness and his ability to read the emotions and dynamics of others around him.

He was struggling to see how it was possible to be an authoritative leader and a 'nice person'. Exploring options for how to use his warmth and emotional intelligence to be authoritative helped Tom to imagine how he could be both. He came to see how to be authoritative without having to be friends.

One of the challenging pieces of feedback from his boss was how Tom shared information. Because he viewed himself as friendly and approachable, he shared information widely. He regularly spoke with a variety of people across the organisation to share the latest news. Tom enjoyed this engagement, and the sense of power that came from passing on the news that others didn't have access to.

What Tom hadn't realised was that this behaviour was compromising the way he was seen by important superiors. His readiness to share information was contributing to a sense that he *overshared*. Through the coaching engagement, his boss related a concern that Tom may be disclosing information that he shouldn't – in other words, gossiping. A potential breach of trust was identified.

The shock associated with this feedback was helpful for Tom to reframe the relationships that were important to him and why. He was able to identify that his need for warmth and friendliness was misfiring. He had to own up to his own status and power needs here: what he saw as his source of power – providing information to others – was a way of maintaining his status. He not only hadn't labelled it that way, he hadn't realised that it was counterproductive.

As the case study shows, viewing authority as different from status opens up the idea that it could come from willingness to self-authorise. Tom realised that he'd mixed up his ideals. He could be much less 'friendly', yet still be warm and engaging. Giving up the need to be friends meant more opportunity to take up authority, and he could exercise his authority in a way that was congruent with the leader he wanted to be.

Tom reflected on what had changed. *'I had some breakthrough thinking. I was not allowing myself to get comfortable with exercising my authority. I was still wanting to be friends. I was wanting to 'not be like x', and that, I can see now, just seems to be backward thinking.*

'Some unconscious things have been released about my relationship to authority. I can engage in a much clearer way; I'm calling people out.

'Having a strong focus on accountability and execution means that I've given myself authority to move into this space. I'm holding boundaries in a much more overt way. I am stepping in and being authoritative. I can do this and maintain my warmth. And I don't have to worry about whether anyone likes me. In fact, I've improved the trust that people have in me, and that is more important. This is a better me, and what I want to be known for it.'

Through coaching we were able to get a better view on whose perspectives Tom was taking. Coaching continued Tom's development from the Socialised to the Self-authoring form of mind. Reacting against the authority figure he didn't like kept him bound by that perspective on authority. Letting go of the resistance helped him to develop a more congruent sense of his own authority. Coaching helped his thinking to become more flexible. He was able to take multiple perspectives openly without feeling internal conflict.

If this area is of particular interest to you, I encourage you to read Jennifer Garvey Berger's books.

It's important to remember, no one form of mind has any greater value than any other, except insofar as it serves you well.

Activity

1. How easy do you find it to take the perspectives of others?
2. Referring to Figure 3.1 and the earlier discussion, which form of mind do you think you take?
3. What is your own comfort level with exercising your own authority? Where do you experience limits to how you exercise authority?
4. What space do you leave your team to act on their own authority?
5. What connection, if any, can you see between your comfort level and the space you leave your team?

The what: a continuum to focus your development

The *Know, Do, Believe, Be* continuum (see Figure 3.2 opposite) offers a practical way of deciding what to develop.

The logic is that learning starts with knowledge. You've probably devoted a lot of your development time to knowing your area of technical expertise. Once you know how to do something, you build your expertise through practice. You build mastery in particular skills.

Figure 3.2 – The Know, Do, Believe, Be continuum

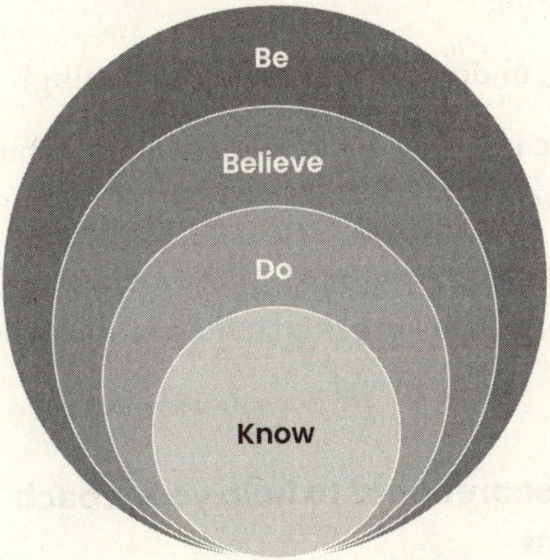

Beliefs or mindsets play a role in learning. How do your beliefs affect what you learn and develop mastery in? What do you believe about what leadership or coaching is?

These then build to 'being'. This level of learning is associated with identity – who you are and who you want to become. When your knowledge, skills and beliefs are congruent with your sense of identity, you have achieved the desired state of 'unconscious competence'.

Turns in the leadership pipeline mean that different knowledge, skills and attitudes are required at different stages of your development. As you move into more senior leadership roles, your identity may need to adapt for you to be successful. If your sense of identity is very strong, you may find it more difficult to imagine yourself as suitable for some roles. Alternatively, you may find it more difficult to adapt into them.

Ask yourself:

- What do I need to *know* to improve my coaching?
- What skills do I have and what do I need to learn so that I '*do* coaching'?
- What do I, or don't I, *believe* about coaching?
- What have I already mastered? What does it mean to me to *be* a coach?

Use the scoreboard discussed in the next section to answer these questions. Then use this frame as a tool when you coach others.

The how: a scoreboard to help your coach development

A learning scoreboard is like the dashboard in your car. It helps you to keep the destination in mind, to calibrate your learning needs, check your speed and record your progress. It's also a tangible way to take accountability for your learning.

The learning scoreboard provides you with a guide for what to focus on as you develop your coaching capability. Charting progress against the four levels of learning will help you to accelerate your development.

Know how to coach

Where do you start? Do you know how to coach, but are not sure about when to coach? Are you coaching everyone, or just some team members? Do you focus on strengths as well as deficits? Is your coaching limited to team members, or do you use your coaching style with peers and other stakeholders?

Knowing how to coach, when to coach and who to coach is a good starting point. Two key issues to bear in mind are:

1. **Beware cognitive overload:** Many leaders experience cognitive overload in their day-to-day work. A busy workload plus a learning program increases the degree of difficulty. Work through these activities in smaller chunks, rather than large ones. Use your calendar so that you remind yourself to participate in small learning acts at regular intervals. Use the reminders to keep your momentum going. This will help you to learn more and to retain your new knowledge and skills.
2. **Separate coaching from performance management:** Distinguish coaching from performance management as far as possible. There are multiple opportunities for coaching. Use coaching skills to help reduce the threat and negativity of performance management-based activities. You will be more receptive to finding opportunities to coach and your team will be more receptive to being coached.

Keep your focus on the positive. If you associate coaching with positive experiences it will strengthen your resolve to coach.

Corridor conversations, micro-coaching conversations and collaborative discussions are all great options for coaching. Focus on ensuring quality conversations, which better align with a coaching culture. This will also provide a positive experience to the person being coached.

Do coaching

Practise coaching behaviours and conversations, as this grows mastery and confidence. *Practise, practise, practise.* To avoid the perception that coaching employees is risky, create opportunities for practise. Get feedback from trusted peers if you can. Find opportunity for reflection and refinement of your own practice of coaching.

Be coached. When leaders themselves are coached, the likelihood that they will coach others increases[16]. It also increases the support they provide to their teams. They delegate more, micromanage less, pay more attention to employees' developmental needs, and put effort into creating a positive and engaging work environment. Reciprocal coaching between peers who are learning together is a powerful way to embed learning into practice. Who might you partner up with?

Believe in coaching

You've probably made it to this point in this book because you have some level of belief in the value of coaching. What are your unanswered questions about its value?

A coaching style won't be right for every situation. But it's right for more situations than you think.

Keep your learning focused on what's relevant to you. How does it help you to do your work? Use it to gain insight into the challenges you face. How might coaching help you to achieve *x*? This leads to new perspectives and solutions, which is energising.

Be a coach

Being a coach fits well with being a good leader. This next case study highlights how Alex thinks about her identity as a leader who coaches.

Coaching as a way of being

For Alex, coaching is a way of being. She consistently receives great feedback on her ability to build relationships and trust. She gets her highest satisfaction from seeing others improve. She says that her job description has never got in the way of who she is meant to be. *'The greatest gift that a leader can bring is to be themselves, to be authentic, to not try to be anything else. I'm bringing my whole self in, and I'm looking at the whole person.'*

She says: *'When someone comes to me with a problem, it's never the problem. I can't tell them what the problem is. I know that if I ask enough questions they will be able to identify their problem. You can see it when they get there, when they land on the problem and can see it clearly. When they work out what is impacting them, they can then take the right action to get on with things. It's really important to be able to dig in and ask questions about what sits behind the initial approach. The only person with the answer is the person who came to you with the problem; your job is to help them to find it.*

As the coach, you need to let go of the need to be right, and to have all the answers. This is hard, because people expect you to have all the answers. This creates an internal conflict. My approach is to relax and play with curiosity. Curiosity is my biggest learning in moving towards coaching. I ask questions to be curious and then let go the need to be right. I need to remove my 'self' from this. When I do, I have amazing breakthroughs with people.'

My last piece of advice here is to find a peer to learn with. A collaborative learning context makes learning much more supportive. It increases trust and provides opportunities for feedback. Who might your partner be? This is the most rapid way to take you from 'do' to 'be'.

Activity

Create the first version of your learning scoreboard. What are your 90-day goals? Use the template below. It will help you to complete this activity. You can also download the template from https://karenmorley.com.au/leadlikeacoach.

1. What knowledge do you need to focus on?
   - How to coach?
   - Who to coach?
   - How, when, where to practise your coaching?
2. What skills do you need to focus on?
3. What attitudes and beliefs do you need to focus on?
   - What's the value of coaching?
   - What would it take for you to coach more?
4. What part of your 'being' or identity as a coach do you need to focus on?

	Readiness to coach	**Self-assessment**	**My development focus**
Know	How to coach When to coach Who to coach		What I want to know:
Do	Experience being coached		What I want to do:
Believe	The value of coaching My ability to coach		What I want to believe in:
Be	Collegial Reflective Open		What I want to be:

Note: The frameworks and tools presented here and throughout the book apply to you as you develop your coaching. They apply equally well as tools when you coach your team.

A word (or two!) on the value of reflection

Reflection is central to growing. Reflect regularly on your emerging coaching practice to increase its benefit. Each piece of practice will have greater value if you pause and reflect on what you did, how it worked and what you learnt.

Reflection is like the fertiliser that fuels the growth of plants. Fertiliser is vital for the plant to flourish. Reflection will similarly help your coaching practice to flourish.

This learning cycle (see Figure 3.3) emphasises four elements[17]. The first is to make sense of new information. The second is to plan and decide how you will use it. The third, to put it into action, and the fourth to observe and reflect on what happens.

Figure 3.3 – The four elements of the learning cycle

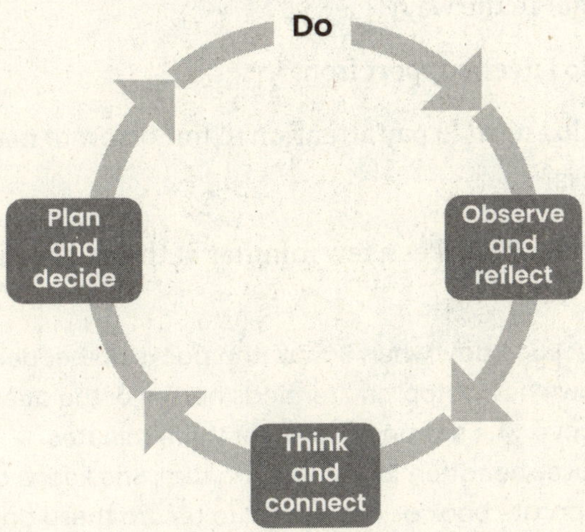

For most of us, the observe and reflect element is the hardest. We are primed to act quickly and to solve problems immediately.

Learning requires us to interrupt the pattern of planning and doing, to reflect and consider new ideas.

If reflecting doesn't come naturally to you, how can you make it easier?

You could try chunking goals and new moves down to the specific behaviours you can practise each day. This seems to be the most effective way to embed change. And noticing 'small wins' is powerful in keeping the motivation for change present[18]. (See Chapter 10 for more about this.)

How can the time-poor executive pause and reflect effectively? One way is to adopt a daily reflection habit that requires you to regularly ask three to four questions, such as:

- What did I do today to achieve progress on my goals?
- What got in the way?
- Who do I need support from?
- What do I need to pay attention to tomorrow to make progress?

This practice only takes a few minutes at the end of each day.

> **Example:** Each day, when Samantha packs up her desk and shuts down her laptop, she reminds herself of the questions listed above. She sits back down for three minutes and focuses her attention on each in turn. She keeps a small separate book as her journal to record these daily

reflections. This helps her to create a discipline to take these moments to reflect on her day. It also helps her to notice the change she is making through her daily record, which forms a tangible representation of her progress over time. Her reflective journal crystallises just how much progress she is making towards developing her own coaching style.

She reflects on her inner doubts and criticisms about how to coach, noticing the shifts in her satisfaction and perspective. She recognises the degree of transformation she has achieved.

Activity

Try a variety of techniques for reflecting. Use the one introduced above, when at the end of each day you ask yourself these three questions. Keep a record of your daily responses and over time compare your progress.

1. What progress did you make on your coaching development goals today?
2. What got in the way of making progress?
3. What progress do you want to make tomorrow?

For other techniques, go to https://karenmorley.com.au/leadlikeacoach.

Transitioning your leadership identity to 'coach'

This chapter seemed to start off as a simple exercise in setting your goals for coaching. Along the way, it became much more than that.

To close the chapter, let's head back to the beginning, where the focus was on leadership, authority and identity. The discussion so far has been on why, what and how. The second part of how is *how does it feel*?

It might seem a big shift to grow your coaching style to be a key part of how you engage with your team. With that shift comes uncertainty, which is just the opposite of what you want to feel. As the leader, you're meant to be certain, right?

To make a successful leadership identity transition to 'coach' will take a fine balance. Balancing the certainty you have as a leader, with the confusion you have of letting go, may be a challenge.

Some leaders even report that they feel somewhat inauthentic during identity transitions. It's important to make the distinction between certainty and growing to make sense of this feeling. It's confusion. That's not the same as inauthenticity.

During this time, how you see yourself is changing. It might feel a bit like you are in a hall of mirrors. It's as if there is a variety of different mirrors that distort the way you look, making you appear in different ways, depending on where you look. In some mirrors, you loom large, in others you are small and in yet others, you seem to disappear. The different reflections are all you, yet not you, as you transition.

It's normal to feel this wobbliness and distortion. That's part of the process. Figure 3.4 shows the relationships between certainty, confusion and clarity as you transition your identity.

Figure 3.4 – How to transition your leadership identity

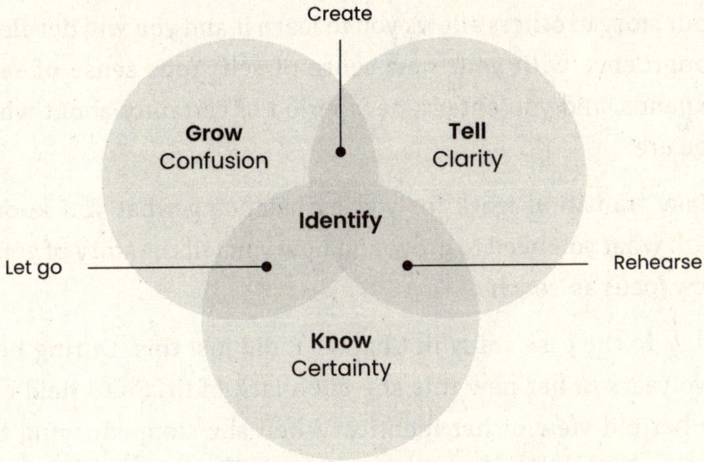

Leadership transitions will create a sense of confusion

Clarity about who you are is disturbed as new challenges arise and different responses are needed. Your identity may be stretched and challenged and that causes the confusion. Your old certainties just aren't as helpful as they used to be. It helps to let go of the need to be certain, if you are to learn how to 'be a new me' in your new context.

It's natural to prefer to have certainty, and to know who we are. To grow, we need to let go of that certainty, but that means experiencing confusion and uncertainty for a period. Through the confusion and the exploration of new ideas and behaviours, we begin to create a new sense of identity.

Exploring new stories about yourself may help you to create clarity, which in turn leads to stronger self-knowledge and a new kind of certainty. The story about your new, emerging, identity will help to sense-check it and further develop clarity.

As this happens and you tell your story more frequently and with more confidence, things become even clearer. Telling your story to others allows you to learn it and you will develop congruence with your new sense of self. Your sense of self expands, and you enter a new period of certainty about who you are.

Make transition work for you by balancing what you know with what you need to grow, and how you tell the story of your new focus as 'coach'.

Amy, in the case study in Chapter 1, did just this. During her two years in her new role she felt a lack of fit. She'd held on to her old view of her identity. When she stopped trying to prove she was the expert (even though she didn't want to be) it was like a gate in her identity was opened. She deliberately told her story to her team. In telling them the story, she gained greater clarity about who she was and how she wanted to lead. It was reinforcing. It opened up new, positive conversations between them.

And Tom, in the case study at the beginning of this chapter, experienced a similar breakthrough. He transitioned into a new role that required him to show greater authority in a highly complex stakeholder environment. *'I don't know the story of what I'm doing'*, was how he described his frustration with himself. His existing skills and perspectives were no longer working for him. His old story about who he was and how to be successful didn't fit the new context.

By focusing on what he knew, what he wanted to grow, and how he could tell others about it, Tom was able to gain clarity through his transition. He became clearer about what was different in the role, and how he needed to be different to succeed in it. By articulating that to others, he was able to clarify his thinking further and it allowed others to understand what to expect from him.

Activity

1. Grow: circle on the continuum below what level of confusion/discomfort arises for you when you focus on doing more coaching:

   None — Very little — A fair bit — Quite a lot — A great deal

2. What do you put that down to?
3. Tell: what is your story about why you are coaching more?
4. Who will you tell your story to?
5. Know: what new clarity about yourself as a leader emerges from your coaching practice and reflection?
6. Grow: what do you need or want to let go of so that you can grow? What have you let go of already?
7. If you experience doubts about your authenticity, what are they?
8. How has your view of your authentic self changed?
9. How has your understanding of authenticity evolved?

Set up your scorecard review cadence

Every 90 days, return to your scorecard and reflect on, review, recalibrate and renew your coach development goals. Figure 3.5 overleaf provides a visual prompt to remind you to do this.

Figure 3.5 – The scorecard review prompt

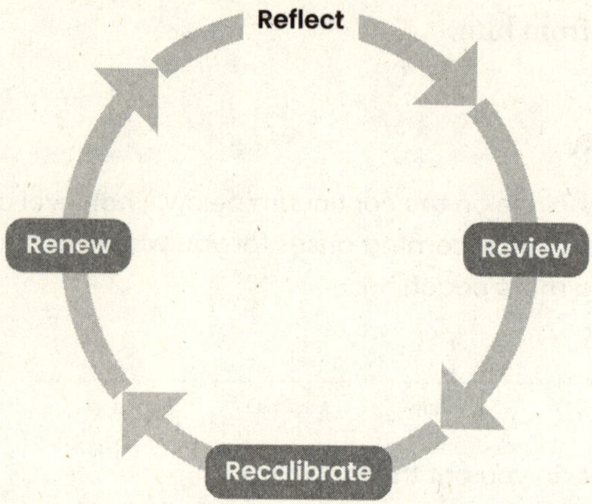

Activity

1. Reflect on your change efforts. What have you learnt? What have you struggled with? What might you need to approach differently? Who has supported your development? Who have you learnt from?
2. Review your progress against your goals. What have you achieved? What have been your successes? What was most helpful to your goal achievement?
3. Recalibrate your goals. What do you need to carry over to the next 90 days? What new goals do you want to add? What's next for your progress?
4. Renew your focus. What are your specific developmental goals for the next 90 days. What support do you need? Who will you seek support from? Update your scorecard.

PART II

Get ready to coach

4

Be like a coach: develop your coaching presence

Coaching is generative. It focuses on how to develop new capabilities, see new horizons and create new opportunities[19]. Outstanding leaders begin with the ideal of generativity. This is the attitude of creating, generating and producing. Their key question is 'How can I grow this person's competence in a way that is respectful and effective?'.

Coaching habits of outstanding leaders

When outstanding leaders coach, they focus on:

- Long-term performance
- Enabling self-correction
- Self-generation.

Long-term excellent performance

When you focus on long-term excellent performance, not just short-term gains, your focus shifts from 'What work needs to get done?' to 'What capabilities does this person need to develop to get this job done?'

One of the simplest ways to do this is to avoid answering when a team member seeks advice. For example, they may ask you 'What do you think?' or 'What's my next step?' Instead of answering, the coaching trick is to ask a question back, for example, 'What have you thought of?' or 'What do you think your next step should be?'

Leaders are primed to know the answer and to respond as quickly as they can. Resisting the temptation to do so can be hard! In fact, what I have observed when training leaders in coaching skills is that the challenge is often just to *notice* that this is happening. Then they can use it as an opportunity. Answering questions is pretty much instinctive. To stop and respond differently takes mindful attention and effort.

You *may* eventually need to answer the question, because your team member just doesn't know. But at least 75% of the time, they either already do know the right answer, or you can help shape the final 25% of their thinking in the right direction to enable them to find the answer for themselves.

Self-correction

Outstanding leaders enable self-correction through insight into their usual patterns of behaviour and their style.

As the coach, you are looking to help your team members get better insight so that they can make their own choices about their behaviour. If they know what their usual patterns are and can see them objectively, they can start to question them. If they understand that there are many different ways to do things, and they are prepared to experiment with some of them, then they learn how to be self-correcting.

Self-correction takes the ability to notice what you do, identify other ways to do it, and then practise the new ways.

Self-generation

Outstanding leaders also develop their own capability to renew, ask questions and let go of unhelpful assumptions[19]. Development is continuous and ongoing. It's not a tick-a-box-and-my-development-is-done kind of thing. It's more about developing capabilities to mastery level. You need to continue to find new capabilities to develop, be ready for the next role before moving into it and develop greater flexibility. This will give you more tools and options to choose from.

Moving from a directive to a coaching style of leadership

Jack had a goal to change his leadership style. He wanted to reduce the amount of time he was in directive mode and increase his use of coaching. He had transitioned into a role where he was now a 'manager of managers'. He realised that he had to change his style to meet the workload demands of the new role. He could not continue to be the expert in everything in his group, nor to know all the detail on everything, as he had in his previous role.

He started answering questions with questions, rather than giving answers. He started one-on-one meetings by asking his team members what was on their minds. He asked them what they wanted to achieve in the meeting, rather than hitting them with a list of demands for information or action.

This was starting to shift the quality of Jack's relationships with his team. He felt very encouraged by the positive responses from most of them. He was feeling some relief from the pressure of trying to know everything.

Jack was frustrated by one of his team, Dan, who often came to him for advice and approval. While Jack's behaviour had changed, Dan's hadn't.

Jack felt that he had created a dependency with Dan who was quiet and self-confessedly rules-oriented. Dan didn't show a great deal of initiative, yet he could be relied on to do his work well and to help other team members when they reached out to him. People trusted him. Having been in his role for about eight years, he was seen as the 'corporate memory' in the team.

Jack realised that to shift Dan's behaviour with him, he needed to help Dan achieve greater insight into his behaviour and style. He realised that there was quite a good fit between his former directive style and the way Dan preferred to be managed. This was making it harder to create change. Jack realised he couldn't just change what he did and expect that Dan would change too.

Jack became more open and explicit with his team about his development. He shared with them what he aimed to do, and how he was doing it. With Dan, he spoke about his changing views on authority and leadership. He shared information on habits of mind with Dan. He invited Dan to reflect on his own development and how he saw authority.

Jack bit the bullet and began to provide more feedback to Dan on how he experienced his behaviours. He used this as a way to begin a discussion about what other behaviours Dan could try. It was a challenge. Jack realised that when he was in coaching mode, it wasn't his role to tell Dan what style he should adopt. He needed to open him up to the variety of style possibilities and allow Dan to choose.

Jack initially self-assessed as being 'Controlling' on the coaching mindset continuum (see Figure 4.1 below). Autocratic and controlling mindsets shut people down. They are not generative and become self-defeating rather than self-generating. A supportive mindset begins and a benevolent mindset accelerates the movement to generativity. The pinnacle of a generative approach is coaching. Jack thought that he was somewhere between supportive and benevolent. His aspiration is to get to 'Coaching'. He wants to be seen as a leader who is a coach and is recognised by others for his coaching style.

Figure 4.1 – The coaching mindset continuum

Jack was inspired by Michelangelo's saying: *'I saw the angel in the marble and I carved until I set it free.'* A coaching mindset looks for the angel in the marble. It looks for the potential within each team member, and then works to help it to be realised.

Activity

1. What is your usual mindset?

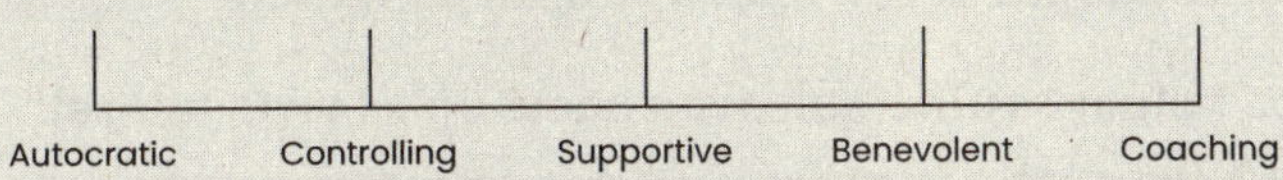

2. What might you do to move closer to, or maintain, a coaching mindset?
3. Consider the individuals in your team. Choose one, Person A, and then consider: How can I grow this

person's competence in a way that is respectful and effective?

- What long-term focus on excellent performance do I need to have?
- How might I enable self-correction (to improve that person's own insight into their patterns and style, and the ability to see their actions objectively)?
- What can I do to support self-generation (to develop that person's own capability to renew, ask questions and let go of unhelpful assumptions)?

4. Complete this exercise for your other team members.

Turning your coaching mindset into action

To be like a coach you need to have a coaching presence. This is how you turn the coaching mindset into action. The mindset is that you actively seek to find, and help to realise, the potential in others. To do this you show them your vulnerability, empathy, humility and appreciation (see Figure 4.2).

Imagine a lake at dawn, when it is calm and still. Imagine the surface of the lake is like a millpond, or like a mirror. The peaceful reflectiveness that it evokes is like a lure. It is as if the world is taking a deep breath. It is an invitation to pause, to sit still and just be. This is an important part of what a coaching presence should be like: calm, still, an invitation.

When you are vulnerable, you show up as your full self. You don't have all the answers, and this offers an invitation to the person you are coaching to mirror you. Warmth and empathy make the connection personal and meaningful.

Figure 4.2 – Elements of coaching presence

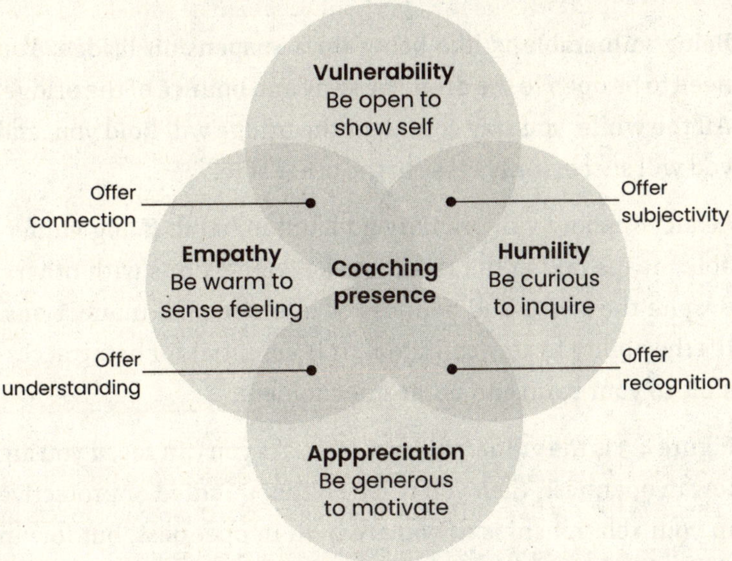

A coach is humble, comfortable asking questions rather than having the answers. This supports the desire to offer, to give, rather than to take.

By being generous with appreciation, a coaching presence helps others to find their motivation to achieve their goals and to continue to develop.

Coaching presence is an offer of recognition, understanding, connection and subjectivity.

Be vulnerable while coaching to increase your connection

If you allow yourself to be vulnerable you will increase personal connection with others in your team. Open yourself to the coaching relationship by giving up your expert/hierarchical power; show up as the real you.

Being vulnerable is like being on a suspension bridge. You need to be open to the drop, the sway and bounce of the bridge. All the while, you stay confident the bridge will hold you, and you will successfully cross to the other side.

Leadership and vulnerability go hand in hand. Being vulnerable means taking the risk to make connections with others, despite the sways and bounces of interpersonal interactions. It's the ability to stay confident. It is essential for being accessible to your team and other stakeholders.

Figure 4.3 is the vulnerability matrix. As you can see, if you are low in openness, then you will be either guarded or protective in your relationships. If you are high in openness, but low in risk, it's like being on a low bridge over an empty stream; it doesn't necessarily advance the relationship.

Figure 4.3. – How to be vulnerable

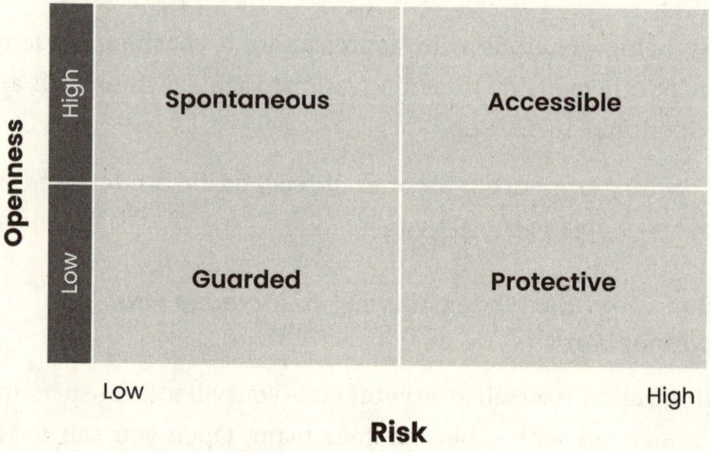

Brené Brown emphasises the importance of vulnerability to meaningful human relationships[20]. Her view of vulnerability is that it is a sign of courage, not weakness. Vulnerability builds human connection, and that's what gives meaning and purpose to our lives. Through your vulnerability as coach you offer connection. You increase your team's opportunity for finding greater meaning and purpose at work.

It takes courage to risk vulnerability. The suggestion here is not to suddenly start disclosing highly personal information. You should not take yourself out on suspension bridges that are too flimsy or poorly anchored.

The number one human piece of coaching is vulnerability. It takes away the myth that the leader is special. It helps to build trust and honesty in the relationship.

> **Example:** To return to Alex's conversation with her engineer colleague: she wanted to know how Alex had been able to appear so confident. Alex shared with her that while she looked confident, she did not feel it. Her view is that to be a great coach you need to show some warts. People will then open up to you, show you their own warts. Alex says, *'She's assumed, and seen me in one way. Then I tell her what was going on inside me. I had voices telling me to shut up, I'm stupid. But I said it anyway.'* The human piece is to share vulnerability.

Showing vulnerability builds trust

Read the context with care. While sharing vulnerability builds enormous trust between people, there needs to be a foundation of trust already. Who do you trust? Who could you trust more than you currently do? How might you explain more about yourself to others, to let them know more about you as a person, your values and aspirations? Start in small ways, with what feels reasonably comfortable, then experiment and expand. This is where I invoke the Goldilocks rule: not too much discomfort, not too little, just the right amount.

Sometimes people confuse vulnerability with weakness. Increased disclosure about your values, motives, reflections and perspectives – your own story – demonstrates strength. It builds trust and is generally very inspiring.

Now consider how vulnerability and leadership are connected.

Activity

1. What does vulnerability mean to you?
2. How do you express your vulnerability?
3. Are you mostly guarded, spontaneous, protective or accessible?
4. What impact does your expression of vulnerability have on you? What impact does it have on others? How satisfied are you with that impact?
5. When you observe leadership role models you admire, how do they demonstrate vulnerability?
6. What would you change about how you demonstrate vulnerability? What might you do more of, less of, stop or start?

Use your empathy to honour the feelings of others

Connecting with people is fundamental to leading them. Your offer of vulnerability starts the process. Next, use your empathy to engage with the other person's experiences and feelings.

Empathy can be lost in the daily pressures of work. There are many distractions, and your attention can be fractured as it is pulled in many directions. To coach, it helps if you can put yourself into the context of the other person, pay attention to them and their experiences. Try to honour their experiences and feelings. Figure 4.4 shows the impact you have on your relationships depending on the perspective you take and your level of emotional awareness. If you stay with your own perspective you will disconnect from or avoid the feelings of others. If you take the other person's perspective you will at least recognise their feelings.

Figure 4.4 – How to create empathy

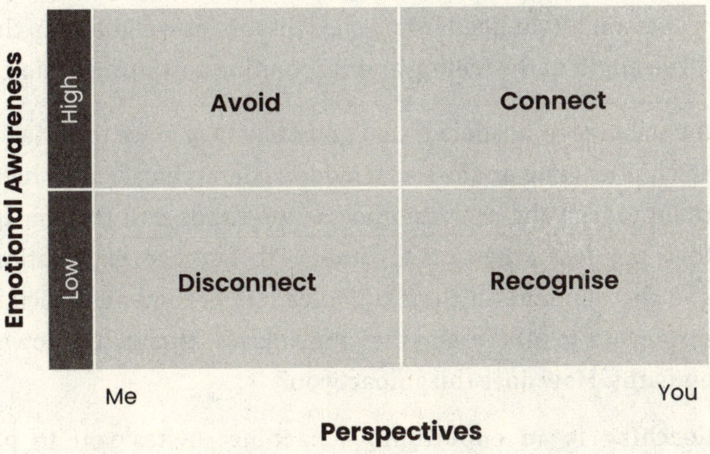

Empathy grows from your ability to take the other person's perspective and have a high level of emotional awareness that allows you to connect with them on a human level.

Empathy is a "human superpower"[21]. It reduces social and power distance, overcomes differences between people and provokes social change. It is vital to any coaching relationship.

Goleman[22] speaks to three kinds of empathy as important for leaders. They are:

1. **Cognitive empathy** – being able to take another person's perspective and to gain a sense of how they are feeling.
2. **Emotional empathy** – being able to feel what another person feels. To do this, you need to read the other person's signals. Then generate an awareness of what they might be feeling, and recall your own experience of that emotion.
3. **Empathic concern** – being able to sense what the other person might need from you. This means weighing up the strength of the feeling and responding with compassion.

A challenge for leaders is that generally they place themselves at a higher rung on the social ladder. Hierarchical status helps them project themselves onto the top rungs. But that means they pay less attention to others. To manage expectations and the demand on their time, leaders become less socially responsive to others, and they tune in less. This in turn lowers empathy. How does this impact you?

Coaching is an opportunity. Coaching invites you to pay more attention to your team members, to tune in to them emotionally and to connect. When people feel listened to and know that they matter, they are more motivated.

Watch Susan David's powerful video of her TED talk on emotional agility[23] to help reflect on how you express your empathy.

Activity

1. How do you rate your own empathy?

   Very low | Quite low | Average | Quite high | Very high

2. What feedback have you had in the past about how you show your empathy?
3. What gets in the way of demonstrating your empathy more?
4. If you show empathy too much, what gets in the way of reducing your empathy?
5. Ask yourself:
   - How well do I understand what motivates people?
   - How sensitive am I to the needs of others?
   - How easily do I attune to the moods of others?
   - How easily do I sense how others feel?
6. In which of these areas could you make an adjustment that would help you improve your empathy and become a better coach?

A humble curious stance lets others be their best

"Humble inquiry is the fine art of drawing someone out, of asking questions to which you do not know the answer, of building a relationship based on curiosity and interest in the other person."[24] These wise words are from Edgar Schein. He has devoted a whole book to humble inquiry. In it he tells this story:

"The other day I was admiring an unusual bunch of mushrooms that had grown after a heavy rain when a lady walking her dog chose to stop and tell me in a loud voice, 'Some of those are poisonous, you know'. I replied, 'I know', to which she added, 'Some of them can kill you, you know'.

"What struck me was how her need to tell not only made it difficult to respond in a positive manner, but it also offended me. I realized that her tone and her telling approach prevented the building of a positive relationship and made further communication awkward. Her motivation might have been to help me, yet I found it unhelpful and wished that she had asked me a question, either at the beginning or after I said 'I know', instead of trying to tell me something more."

Coaching is built on asking questions and avoiding telling the solution. As this story shows, we are predisposed to tell others, rather than to ask. Leaders in particular fall prey to this tendency. Leaders often feel as if they are on a hurtling express train, so sure of their destination, focused only on getting there, on being on time. Relationships, however, need stops along the way. They need curiosity and pauses, and you need to devote time to them. Relationships need reciprocal two-way interaction. They need the slower train, the cadence of asking as well as telling, if they are to flourish.

As the leader-coach, you don't have to be the expert. You can step back from being in 'telling' mode. You're not the expert on the other person. As Figure 4.5 shows, when your curiosity is low and you 'know' the answer, you are most likely to tell. Instead, allow the other person to be the expert on themselves. Switch to high curiosity: ask them. You lead them to find the right answer.

When the answer is unknown or uncertain, if you engage with low curiosity, you will avoid finding out what is possible, or known by others. If you engage with high curiosity – and ask – you find new solutions. A side benefit of a coaching relationship is that you learn too; you learn as much as the person you are coaching.

Figure 4.5 – How to be humble

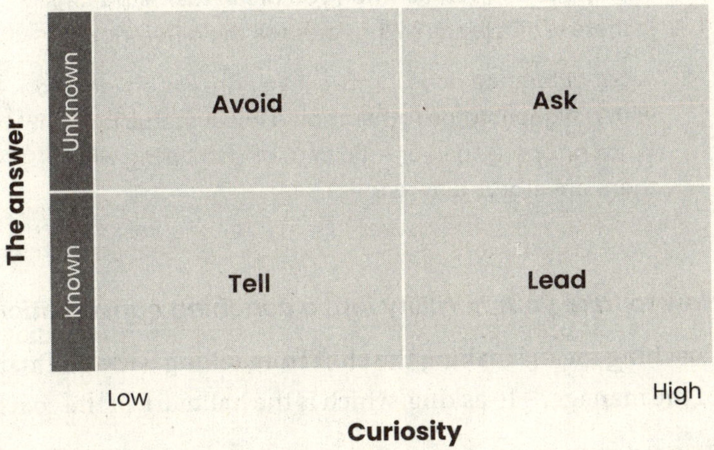

What remains difficult in some organisations is for junior staff to feel safe to bring up a range of issues that need to be addressed. They have information that might reduce accidents and injuries in the workplace, and mistakes that might detract from value for customers. A coaching climate is more likely to create a level of safety for everyone to share information and communicate. It relies on the leader being humble, to have the ability to listen carefully, and to be less certain of having all the answers. When a leader behaves like this, staff are more likely to make out-of-the-box suggestions, and to volunteer contentious information. Such an environment is rarely built where leaders do the bulk of the telling.

Activity

1. What is your ratio of asking questions to telling others what to do?
2. What is the ratio when you are in ordinary, daily conversations, versus when you are in task situations? Is there a difference? What creates the difference?
3. What difference does it make if you are in conversation with a higher status rather than a lower status person? What happens to your ratio of asking to telling when there are status differences?

How to take your humility into a coaching conversation

Coaching means making the shift from telling – the hallmark of the manager – to asking, which is the hallmark of the coach.

You can see a conversation as being like an artist's palette. In your conversation, spread out all the colours on your palette. Choose and mix the different colours into your conversation. This gives it greater light and shade, greater appeal.

Balancing asking with telling on your palette can be difficult to achieve. Asking, when you know, or believe you know, can be especially challenging.

To improve your asking skills, try using these prompts[25]:

- What leads you to conclude that?
- What data do you have for that?
- What causes you to say that?

- Help me to understand your thinking.
- What is the significance of that?
- How does this relate to your concerns?
- Where does your reasoning go next?
- How would your proposal affect...?
- What is this like?

Activity

Think of an upcoming conversation where it would be beneficial to explore your coachee's assumptions. Perhaps you don't understand what the assumptions are or haven't had time to think through their reasoning.

1. Use this checklist and plan how you would have the conversation, to improve your inquiry skills:
    - Explain why you want to know
    - Ask for their reasoning, their why
    - Seek to understand their reasoning
    - Avoid being critical or aggressive
    - Check your understanding
    - Compare points of commonality and difference.
2. When you've had the conversation, come back and reflect on what worked, what didn't work so well, and what you would do next time.

Appreciate others to let them know they matter

Appreciation lets us know that what we do matters. Knowing that we matter connects us to others. When we feel that what we do at work is valuable, it satisfies one of our deepest human needs.

Appreciation tells people that they are valued.

Appreciation grows satisfaction which increases performance and results in people feeling valued, as depicted in this graphic.

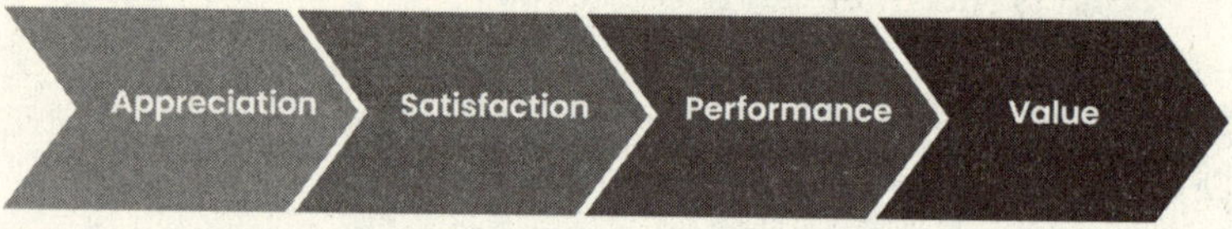

"Regularly producing appreciation is like pumping oxygen into the system", in the words of Kegan and Lahey[26].

Not enough time is spent pumping oxygen into the system. Not enough time is spent letting people know that what they do matters, that they make a contribution that has value, and that they are worthy of being noticed. We spend too much time at work for our contribution to go under-recognised.

Appreciation, if it is expressed well, and genuinely, can make a very big difference.

I commonly hear this phrase: 'You can expect to hear about it if there's a problem.' Sometimes it seems as if there is almost an aversion to saying positive things about others. It makes sense that many of us are averse to the conflict. It is negative, it can be difficult and uncomfortable, and we may fear its potential to disrupt relationships.

It is more puzzling that we under-communicate positive admiration and appreciation towards others. What a paradox this is: feeling appreciated is something that is so fundamental to our wellbeing, but so few of us go out of our way to make others feel appreciated.

If you would like to increase your appreciation-giving, how might you go about it?

Step 1: Tune into actions that are worth appreciating

How do you tune in? You need to set aside your own 'busyness', be mindful and pay attention to others.

What you notice when you do this doesn't have to be a huge event or something even moderately life-changing. It might be a regular day-to-day occurrence that seems pretty insignificant, but it makes a small difference to how your hour or your day goes. Notice what you can.

Step 2: Provide appreciation

Let's focus on giving high value appreciation[26]. Try this now: take 30 seconds to think about a recent experience you have of a team member's behaviour. Imagine that you are going to express your appreciation to this person in an upcoming conversation or meeting. Write down what you would say to them.

Once you've done that, test what you've written. How direct is it? We commonly use indirect language, for example, 'I want to say a word of appreciation to John'. To increase the value of your appreciation speak directly to John, 'I want to say a word of appreciation to *you*'.

How specific is it? We are often general, rather than specific. We talk about how we *felt*, rather than what was *done* that caused us to feel great. For example, 'You did a great presentation to the client yesterday. It is fantastic to be a part of the team with you.' The initial response will be to feel good. Yet, what was done that was great? You might infer that what you did was due to something entirely different from what others noticed.

Be specific about why you thought the presentation was great. Be clear on your own assumptions about what you like. This is as valuable for the person you are appreciating as it is for you. Do you appreciate it when someone completes tasks before they are due, or when they contribute a new idea? What's the pattern to what you notice and appreciate? How balanced are you? As a leader, you direct particular actions by your pattern of appreciation. Does your pattern mean that you over- or under-appreciate particular behaviours or particular people? What's the balance of your appreciation?

Avoid attribution when you express your appreciation. Appreciation that attributes value to certain personality characteristics tends to box the person in – and you may get your attributions wrong.

What could be wrong with saying to someone: 'You have such a great sense of humour'? Perhaps they believe they have a great sense of humour, but perhaps they don't. Perhaps they value humour, but perhaps not. Perhaps they don't want to be seen as the joker, they would prefer to be taken seriously. In that moment, being told by you what they are could feel limiting. And if that's repeated over time, the attribution may become unhelpful.

'You' statements tend to provoke a reaction, sometimes even defensiveness. 'I' statements that focus on my own experience of your behaviour, don't. 'I enjoyed your comment. It was very helpful because it relieved some of the tension that was building up. Our conversation was becoming very intense and it felt like we were stalling. What you said helped us to lift our heads a bit and go back into the conversation with more energy, and a different focus. We were able to move forward.' This approach works equally well for positive and negative statements.

Appreciation that is about the experience of what you have done, rather than an attribution of what you are, has the greatest value. When I know how you experience what I do, I will feel most valued.

Step 3: Make it a habit

Incorporate appreciation into your coaching style and help others to feel good about the contribution they make. Help them to thrive.

Activity

1. How often are you likely to appreciate the work of your team?

Rarely	Now and then	Monthly	Weekly	Daily

2. What needs to change for you to give appreciation more often?
3. What might go wrong?
4. Prepare some direct, specific appreciation, based on your own experience, for each of your team members.

Coaching presence is based on vulnerability, empathy, humility and appreciation. To be like a coach, identify your strengths and the areas you need to develop. What do you need to improve to have a coaching mindset and bring out the full potential of your team and each member of it?

5

Believe in your power to coach

Being a better coach means setting aside the need to be an individual contributor. It means leaving behind the control and status of management to focus on being the leader of the team. With a coaching mindset, your focus is to enable the team and each individual team member to grow to their full potential. That's your most important contribution.

Put others first

Lee had been a first line manager for a while and had worked hard on her own personal development. Her hard work paid off when she was appointed to a senior manager role. Now she was a manager of team leaders who were managing their own teams.

She had put so much personal effort into this accomplishment. She was pleased to have the status that the role afforded, and to be recognised for her capabilities. She was now in a role that allowed her to work with the peers she saw herself as equal to. She felt like basking in the recognition; her personal satisfaction was high.

Yet she realised early on that she needed to make a choice about how she wore her status. She could wear the status and power that came with the new role as her own, or she could share it.

She quickly made her choice and decided she would aspire to share her status and her power. She described this as making the choice between being a manager and holding the status, or being a leader and sharing it with others. She then set herself the challenge to make her leadership legacy one of putting her team first.

Coaching is the leadership style that does this best. By coaching you are giving practical care and support to your team. Coaching focuses on each team member – on their needs, their interests, their suggestions and their development. It comes from a place of genuine inquiry. It helps them to feel valued and appreciated. When you care for your team members, they know. When they know you care, they care more about their work and work harder. They are more motivated and more satisfied.

Coach the person, not the problem

When you're playing football, to play well, you need to keep your eye on the ball. Where the ball is, and what's happening to the ball, helps you identify what the next play should be. In coaching, keeping your eye on the ball translates to keeping your eye on the person, not their problem.

Coaching focuses on the person, or coachee. What are their needs, interests and suggestions? It comes from a place of humility and genuine inquiry.

Coaching is not about solving someone's problem for them but helping them to be able to solve their own problems.

First, when you coach, you need to understand the person's context (see Figure 5.1). You need to hear how they construct and make sense of their problem.

Figure 5.1 – The coaching focus

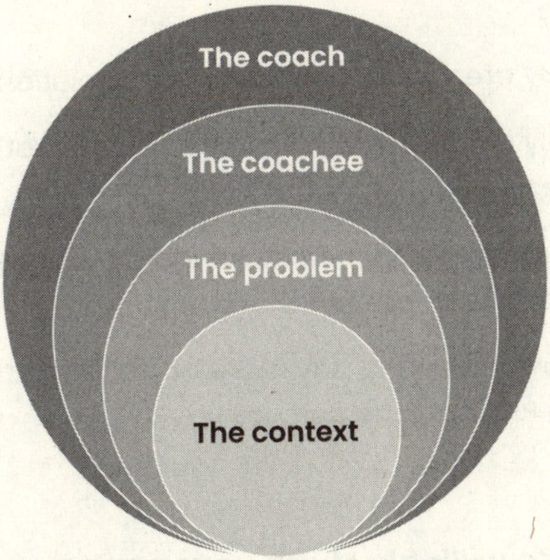

In between the problem and you, there's the coachee. Listen deeply to what the coachee says about the problem. Avoid offering advice and suggestions. Ask how they see their problem. What have they tried to do about their problem? Where are they stuck? Is this where they always get stuck? What's the barrier to finding their own solution?

Most leaders find it hard to avoid automatically naming the solution. Your task as coach is not to find the solution. You might already know the solution – or at least one of them – but hold back and help the person find their own.

Example: Lee's challenge is to avoid sharing what she believes is the solution to the problem as soon as she identifies it. After all, that's what she was good at in her last role. But she's in a new role now and needs to adopt a new approach. Her attention must stay focused on what her team members need to think about and to learn. That way they will be able solve their own problems and develop their future capability.

Activity

1. How likely are you to jump straight to solution mode?
2. How likely is it that you will offer a solution rather than ask questions and coach?
3. How easily are you able to distinguish between the person and their problem?
4. What do you need to pay more attention to, to ensure that you focus on the person?

To coach is to willingly share your power

Coaching shifts the power dynamic between leader and the team, making it more equitable and empowering for everyone.

Many of us feel uncomfortable discussing power. Yet leaders need to learn to be comfortable with the exercise of power. If you are a leader who wants to bring out the best in others, and be both powerful and good, understanding more about power dynamics may help. In the example above, what Lee decided to do by minimising status distinctions and prioritising coaching was to grant her power generously.

In the example below, a leader is demotivated by the way his boss uses her power. It shows how the misuse or lack of awareness of power dynamics can derail relationships.

Tuning in to the impact of power on others

Power became an obstacle for Michael. He became frustrated with his boss. He thought she had misunderstood his actions dealing with a tough situation. He felt angry and unsupported.

Michael was very pleased with how he had handled a challenging relationship issue in his team. The backstory is that he had inherited a poorly performing team. He worked hard to retrieve the business and turn the culture around. His view was that he had taken very different action with a difficult team member compared with what he would have done in the past. It had worked out unexpectedly well. Some tough feedback was given and accepted. Behaviour had improved. The difficult team member was now showing significant positive change. A weight had been lifted from his shoulders.

Job well done... Or was it?

In the past, his boss had called him out for how he had handled challenging relationship issues. In an ocean of exceptional feedback about performance, this was the one bit of flotsam that marred his reputation.

Michael was floored by his boss's response. The feedback was that he handled this challenge in the same way as past challenges – not well. He felt dismayed. Frustratingly, it seemed that his present actions were not seen as different.

From floating on his tide of success and relief, the comments from his boss had plunged him into the murky depths of self-doubt. He was puzzled. He felt exposed and unsupported. The boss had swept aside the progress he had been making on this key issue.

In the case study above, Michael's emotional reaction was strong. Why? In our coaching conversations, we followed several streams of thinking. How useful was Michael's response? We talked about being hooked (see more about unhooking in the next chapter). What had the boss actually said? How could the boss not see the change? Did the boss not see the change? Was Michael himself using the old meme about his conflict response to filter the feedback from the boss in an unhelpful way?

Why did Michael give so much weight to his boss's perception?

What ensued was a conversation about power. *'Power is a dirty word', Michael said. 'It makes me feel uncomfortable and I don't like it when people use their power in a bad way.'*

It is surprisingly easy for leaders to underestimate how powerful their small comments can be. They lose sight of how others experience their power. How can leaders be more aware of the impact of their power, and use their power for good?

Bad is stronger than good

One area in which leaders can take greater care is in the proportion of positive to negative experiences they emphasise. Taking care with the relative balance of feedback (see more on feedback in Chapter 9) is important because bad is stronger than good[27] – almost always.

Bad events and negative feedback have much more impact than good. Negative information is processed more thoroughly. So, it gets into our heads more easily, and we retrieve it more readily.

When bosses focus on what's wrong, what didn't work, what hasn't changed, it sticks.

Leaders can overcome bad, in favour of good, by:

1. **Force of numbers.** Balance positive examples to outweigh the negative (yes, that old trick still has merit).
2. **Active suppression of the bad news** and cultivation of positive stories. Avoid repeating the bad times and bad news; make sure you cultivate a favourable overall view.

Individuals can overcome bad in favour of good, by doing (1) and (2) as much as they can, and adding (3) or (4):

3. **Don't take it personally, even if it feels personal.** Try to distance yourself from the attributions.
4. **See the negative attributions as unimportant.** If the individual believes that there is a pattern of goodness, they are more likely to disregard the bad.

It may be difficult for individuals to downplay leaders' attributions, due to status differences. This was the case for Michael in the earlier example.

Rethinking power

The boss's construction of events has greater power because of status differentials. Some bosses wield their power with greater insight and care than others. Individuals respond to the boss's power in different ways.

There were a multitude of micro-exchanges of power between Michael and his boss. He felt powerful providing his boss with an update on what he had experienced as challenging. He had considered broader sensitivities from those that concerned him. He took a different approach. He felt proud of handling the situation well.

And, with one small comment from the boss, he experienced wipe-out. He felt overpowered and diminished.

The boss is likely unaware of the impact of her comments – at least partly because she is unaware of the currency of her own power. It's a bit like she's dealing in US dollars, while Michael is working with the Aussie dollar. Her power is of a different currency, and it has a different value. A little of her power is actually quite a lot.

The power paradox

As the leader–coach you want to do good with the power your status brings. The approach to power that Dacher Keltner[28] proposes will help. He turns our traditional view of power as Machiavellian on its head.

Keltner has researched and written about what he calls 21st century power. He suggests we need to move away from traditional, commonly held ideas of power. Machiavelli's beliefs, that you gain power by force or undermining others, are out of date. Keltner's research indicates that power operates in a different way. It shows that, in everyday life, power isn't gained and held by force and coercion.

Instead, power has the greatest value when used generously. Influence is gained, and held, by granting power to others (see Figure 5.2). Coercive force, or the heavy-handed use of power, doesn't influence. Influence comes from empowering others through granting them power.

Having power can be very seductive. Power exists in all human relationships. Lasting influence doesn't come from grabbing power. Doing so provides you with a 'power high', rather than a 'generosity high'. People can only 'grab' power for so long before it has a negative effect on their reputation.

Figure 5.2 – The impact of power

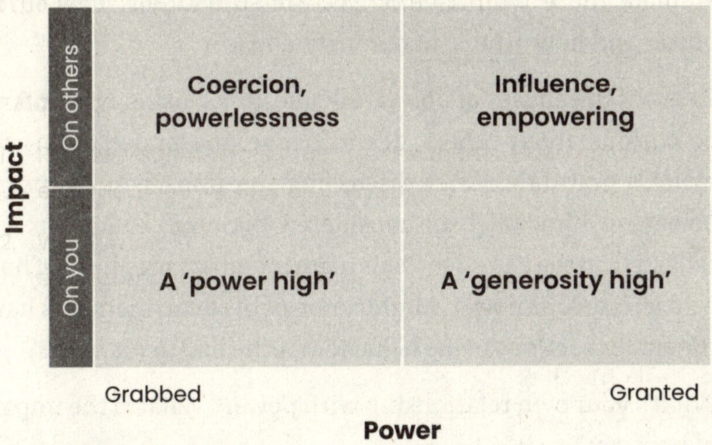

We gain power, experience the 'power high', become seduced by it, abuse our power, and then lose it. This is what Keltner calls the "*paradox of power*". He redefines power as a process of granting it. By granting power, we empower others and it is through this that we gain influence.

You can grant your power, and empower others if you:

- are aware of your feelings of power;
- practise humility;
- stay focused on others and their interests;
- practise respect; and
- work on eliminating powerlessness.

If you are a leader and you want to bring out the best in others and be both powerful and good:

- Focus on the positive and minimise the negative; and
- Grant your power generously.

We may become seduced by others with power and seek to emulate those who have it. We are sometimes repelled by power and how others, in our view, abuse it.

To avoid the abuses of power, ask questions, listen with intent, be curious about others, acknowledge and praise them and express gratitude. After discussing the impact of his boss's power on him, Michael considered his own leadership. He reflected on the experience his team members may have of how he exercised his power. Might some of his team members have the same reactions to his behaviour as he had to his boss's?

What's your own relationship with power? What is the impact of how you use it?

Activity

1. Be aware of power. How do you use your power? Do you grab it or grant it?
2. How does power affect you over time?
3. How do others in your organisation use their power? Do they grab it or grant it? And what is their impact?
4. How do you practise humility and avoid the seductions and the revulsions of power?
5. How do you stay focused on others? How does that play out for you in coaching relationships?
6. What do you do to bring out the good in others?
7. How do you show your respect when you are coaching? What might you do to increase how you show your respect?

Moderate your need for status and dominance

How easy or difficult is it for you to grant your power generously to others? If you have a high need for status and have a dominant personality, how well do you moderate these needs?

Taking into account the discussion of power above, add to it a consideration of your own need for status and dominance.

Status comes with leadership roles: we expect a degree of dominance. Displays of dominance create the impression of having leadership potential. We expect leaders to take charge, to know the answers, to jump in.

Leadership is a fine balance of demonstrating these requirements, while not overdoing them. Be mindful of how much you dominate. How much room do you leave for others?

Displays of dominance include talking more often and at a higher volume. They include using more expansive gestures, such as chin thrusting, and using sharper, explosive hand gestures. These gestures all take up more space and may move into the space of others. When you take up more space, there is less room for others (see Figure 5.3).

Figure 5.3 – Coaches share their space

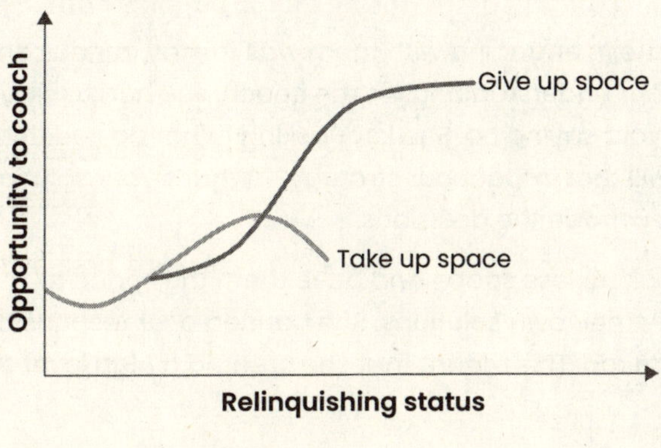

If you can get onto the same level as them, people will respect you. In the following case study Alex uses vulnerability to take away the myth of the leader as special.

Coaching from the same level

Alex doesn't want people to look up to her, she wants to be on their level to create a deep human connection. The respect she enjoys from her teams is very high. She spends time with her teams going about their work, understanding the challenges of their work, and the mundane character of some of it.

When Alex became leader of a large call centre, her people were disenfranchised. Her company had won awards for their culture, yet this part of the business didn't share the same success. The teams felt that they weren't listened to and that they were second-class citizens.

Alex reviewed their culture results. She coached the teams through a series of conversations. She told the teams that she had heard what the problems were and that she wanted to fix them. She said that she couldn't fix the problems, they needed to. Her role was to facilitate the solutions, but the solutions needed to come from them. She put in specific boundaries, and then it was up to them to identify what to do.

Her state in engaging with them was to stay curious and to show her understanding. As the coach, she had to sit back and avoid saying no. She kept asking 'What do you think?' 'How will that impact our strategy?' 'What's your solution?' So, *they* made the decisions.

She took up less space and gave them the space to identify their own solutions. She handed over responsibility to them too. This meant that she created a high level of engagement in the change process. The teams created changes in the areas that were most meaningful to them and they owned the changes. Alex empowered them. The actions helped the teams to feel like they were first – not second – class citizens.

Opportunities to coach arise when you take up less of the space. To coach, give up your space and relinquish your status to the person you are coaching.

Activity

1. What is your natural tendency to take charge, control resources and pursue status?
2. How hierarchically oriented are you?
3. To what extent are you driven by the need for status?

Not all	Very little	A fair bit	Quite a lot	A great deal

4. How will you check how much space you take rather than give?

Stop managing, start coaching

Be clear about the distinction between coaching and other forms of engagement. Coaching requires a different focus and use of power. Be clear about these distinctions to make it easier to coach (see Figure 5.4 overleaf).

Figure 5.4 – Differences between coaching, mentoring, managing and consulting

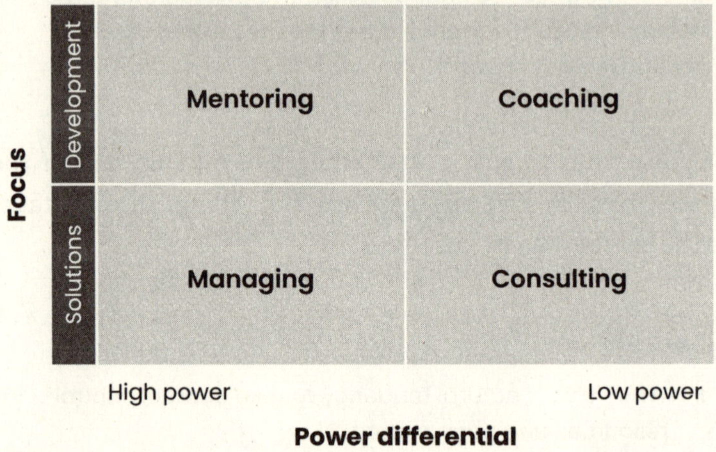

Coaching is the leadership mode that puts others first. This makes it different from managing, consulting and mentoring. They are all legitimate ways of engaging. Each engages power differently and has a different focus for the interaction.

Mentoring is development-focused, like coaching, but there is a bigger difference between the mentor's and the individual's expertise. Both managing and consulting are solutions-focused.

Coaching reduces the power differential and focuses on development, not solutions. It's not just external coaches who coach. And it's not just leaders who coach. It's a style of engaging that anyone might use.

Team members might coach each other, they might coach their boss, as well as be coached by him or her.

To transition between the different styles, prime yourself to put on a different cap. The metaphorical cap reminds you to adjust the power differential and your focus.

Activity

1. Mentor, coach, manager, consultant: which is your default mode?
2. How focused are you on solutions (rather than development) with team members?

None	Very little	A fair bit	Quite a lot	A great deal

3. Dial your power down. Use a metaphor like a coaching cap as a way to prime yourself before you coach. How will you prime yourself to take a coaching approach?

Pay it forward: develop next-gen leaders

When leaders take a generative approach with their team, and put the coaching cap on, they grow future leadership capability.

Sometimes it's necessary to take a pass on the opportunity to show that you know the answer. Instead, help someone else to learn. Do this on a continuing basis. You are not just teaching your team how to learn and to sustain their own growth. You are developing their autonomy, independence and initiative.

Help your team to develop the capability they will need in their next roles, before they move into them. And strengthen talent and leadership in your organisation.

Activity

What support or challenge can I give right now that will help my team members to develop their future capability?

Delegate to grow trust

Part of developing next generation leaders is to delegate, to give up status and power in the service of your team members, and this relies on trust. We have already talked about trust earlier in the book, but here I look at it in the context of relinquishing power and delegating as part of your coaching.

The paradox is that research tells us that leaders aren't confident to coach if a trusting relationship doesn't exist. They judge it to be too risky, and they worry about possible adverse reactions. As a consequence, they miss simple, positive opportunities to coach[2]. And they miss the opportunity to further develop their coaching skills and confidence.

This is a bit of a chicken and egg situation. If trust doesn't exist, the chances of coaching are low. Yet coaching grows trust.

First, a definition of trust: trust is a word often used, and it means different things to different people. To keep it simple, trust has two main aspects. The first is a willingness to be open to someone else's actions. The second is a positive expectation that the other person will not exploit the situation for him or herself[11].

As with Amy's experience (see case study in Chapter 1), preparedness to delegate is a good proxy for trust. Delegation shows that you are willing for someone else to take responsibility. You show you are open. You have a positive expectation that there will be no exploitation. You expect work to get done.

How much do you delegate? Think of each act of delegation as like a ripple in a pond. You create the first drop, and the first ripple. The ripples continue, momentum grows, and trust increases with each ripple.

Delegation is the proof of trust for team members.

People assess how much you trust them by how much you delegate to them.

Delegation is perceived as reward

Team members experience delegation as a reward, which increases trust[12].

When expectations and trust are low, people stagnate. When expectations are low and trust is high, then protection results (see Figure 5.5). Protection may be a safe place, but it prevents growth and development.

Figure 5.5 – The relationship between expectations and trust

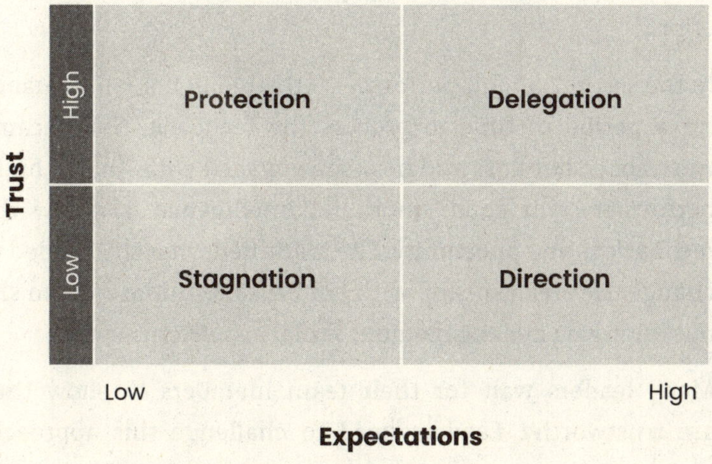

When expectations are high but trust is low, the best result is a directive, commanding leadership style. When expectations are high and trust is also high, then the conditions for delegation are perfect.

Contrast this feedback, provided by the same line manager, to two of his direct reports.

Example 1: *'He pushed me to do the presentation to the board. I said I wasn't ready. He said he thought I was. He asked me, what can he do to support me? ... After the presentation, his feedback blew me away. He trusts me, I'm getting so many opportunities, I feel like I'm in a really good space.'*

Example 2: *'I have not been able to stop thinking about the feedback from my manager. That he doesn't feel he can trust me with information has really rocked me. I know now why I am not getting some of the opportunities that I think I should.'*

In the first example, the impact of the trust was to create huge motivation and commitment. It spurred greater discretionary effort.

In the second, a high-performer retreated in her performance for a period of time to process the feedback. She became wary about her boss and how she engaged with him. A high-performer with good emotional intelligence, she saw the feedback as an opportunity. She identified what she needed to change. Her relationship with her boss has improved and she has improved her engagement skills.

Many leaders wait for their team members to show they are trustworthy. Leaders need to challenge this approach.

Where leaders trust first, team members are more likely to reciprocate.

Don't wait to see trust before you delegate. Delegate and see trust grow. Put your caution aside and offer trust to generate trust.

Activity

1. How much trust have you created in your relationships with team members?

   None | A little | A fair bit | Quite a lot | A great deal

2. How much do you currently delegate to your team?

   Nothing | A little | A fair bit | Quite a lot | A great deal

3. If you trust and delegate in different amounts, what impact do you think that has on your team?
4. What prevents you from trusting first?
5. What could you do to improve your delegation and increase your trust?

Coaching signals genuine caring and grows trust

The coaching style supports and reinforces trust through delegation. Leaders have three levers to work with to grow and maintain trust, and to repair breaches. These are competence, benevolence and integrity[13] (see Figure 5.6 overleaf).

Figure 5.6 – The three levers of trust

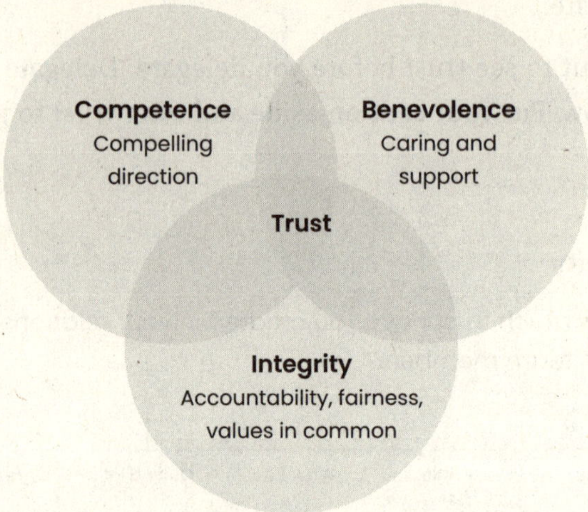

Leaders show competence by setting a compelling direction. They create enabling structures for work (such as work design, allocation of resources and team norms).

Expert coaching by the leader conveys benevolence. It signals genuine caring and support. The more people experience their leader as caring and supportive, the deeper the trust. Through coaching, team members provide input and suggestions, and this helps them to feel valued and appreciated. Only about one-fifth of people feel that they get feedback from their boss that helps them to do better work. About the same proportion feel they are managed in a way that motivates them to do outstanding work[29].

When people perceive their leaders to be benevolent, they are more likely to reciprocate. They work harder for longer and are more likely to go above and beyond what's required.

Air cover is a key part of support. When team members encounter difficulties or challenges, leaders support and protect them. Team members will know that you 'have their backs'. Later, difficulties can be debriefed as learning opportunities rather than mistakes[30].

Finally, integrity means being accountable by doing what you say you will do, treating people fairly, and having values in common.

Activity

1. How do you show your team that you care about them?
2. What do you think they would say about whether your level of care is enough for them?
3. What prevents you from showing greater benevolence to your team?
4. How/when might you ask your team what support they need?
5. What could you do to make sure you provide air cover for team members? How do you notice when they need air cover? How do they notice when you provide it?

6

Think like a coach

Coaching thinking needs to be flexible. As coach, you need to be able to take different perspectives. Chapter 4 outlined the power of perspective taking for development. This chapter presents ways to increase your thinking flexibility.

Taking different perspectives is a powerful way to open up new possibilities for action[15]. This chapter explores a method for shifting your own perspective. You can use this method to help your coachee to explore different perspectives too.

Being aware of the hooks in your own thinking helps to free up unhelpful thinking patterns. This is part of the ability to create new perspectives. You can be fairer and more inclusive when you coach if you are aware of biases that affect decision making.

Flexibility of thinking helps you to draw distinctions. Distinctions help the coachee to see their context and issues with fresh eyes and to self-generate options for action.

Good coaches know some of the quirks and biases that characterise decision making. They are aware of what holds their own thinking back. They overcome these challenges by taking broader perspectives. They move flexibly between different positions and use their coaching capability to help their team members do likewise.

Coaching requires cognitive flexibility

Leaders need to be able to shift perspectives as they coach, to understand the perspective of the other. How flexible is your thinking?

Cognitive flexibility is like a kaleidoscope, which creates many patterns with the same pieces. Coaches have the curiosity to turn the scope to see new patterns. They can give up existing patterns. They know that there are endless possibilities.

You can be flexible without your thinking becoming fractured or fused if you stay present in the moment, open to experience. Figure 6.1 helps to explain this.

Figure 6.1 – Perspective and cognitive flexibility

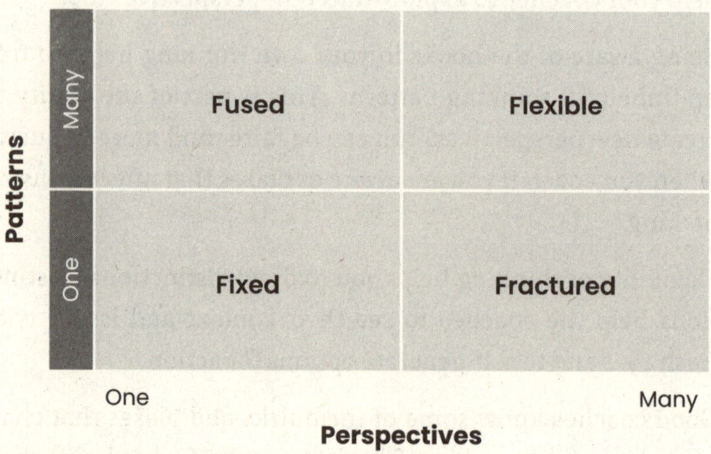

Cognitive flexibility is important in coaching in two ways.

Firstly, it helps you as coach to stay present. You suspend your ego, remaining open to what the person you are coaching says and does. You hear and appreciate their position. You seek to understand their story from their viewpoint. You keep your own views in check.

Secondly, you develop it in others as you coach. You model flexibility. Increasing your flexibility is a way to help your coachee to do the same. They become self-generating and better able to manage their own ongoing development.

Seeking new perspectives

Lan refocused her purpose by imagining her working life from a future perspective.

A couple of years earlier, she decided to move her career in a different direction. Since then she has taken on short-term roles to help make that shift. As the current opportunity came to a close, she felt perplexed at her lack of energy and motivation. For someone usually motivated and excited by her work, this made her very anxious.

Lan admitted that she 'always' thinks from the present to the future. Thinking back from the future perspective to the present was challenging. She drew several 'bubbles' in which she considered various possibilities for her career. Just the opportunity to explore these options helped her to open up her thinking. Lan played with the bubble analogy and came to the decision that this new career path was wrong for her. She 'burst that bubble', but in a good way!

She reflected that she had been somewhat seduced by her success as a good people leader. As a natural extension, that led to the idea of her pursuing a career in human resources. Her realisation was that she could best be an exceptional people leader in senior operational leadership roles. This would be much more satisfying. She was able to craft herself the role she wanted and to re-energise.

Lan flipped her thinking. She used the tactic of thinking from the future back to the present, rather than her habit of thinking from the present to the future. Seeing her context in a new way meant she could consider different options.

Activity

1. Think of a recent interaction you had with one of the people you are coaching.
2. Were you able to stay fully focused on them?
3. Did you remain open to the experience of coaching them? If yes, what helped you to do that? If no, what got in the way?
4. What might you need to do more of, or less of, to improve your flexibility?

How to flexibly position your thinking

Seeing things from others' points of view is like removing a set of blinkers – whole new vistas can be seen.

One way to do this is to be able to flexibly move between first, second and third positions. These are three key perspectives from which to pay attention to information.

Each position represents a way to view the world from a different perspective (see Figure 6.2):

- In first position (I), your attention is focused on your own subjective experience;

- In second position (You), your attention is focused on another person's view of the world (including how they view you); and
- In third position (We), your attention is focused on neutral observation.

Figure 6.2 – Three different perspectives

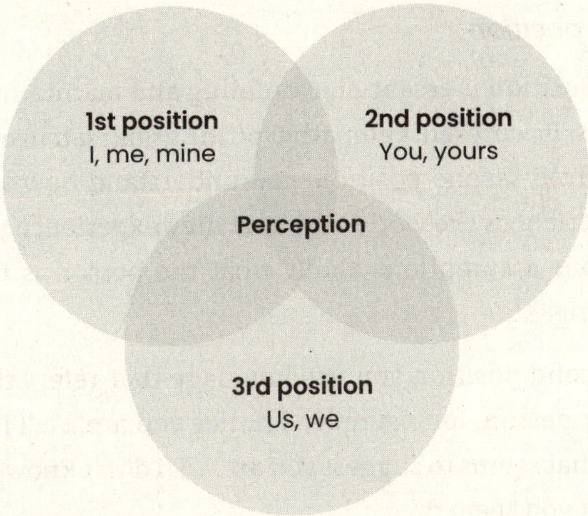

First position

In first position, you experience the world through your own eyes. First position focuses your attention on your inner experience, on how you think and feel about your ideas and experiences. From first position, you focus on you.

First position relies on language that refers things back to you, for example, 'I feel… ', 'I think… ', 'My opinion about that is… ', 'You are wrong about that… ', 'What I would do in that situation is… '.

Operating predominately from first position restricts your ability to form relationships. You focus on what matters to you to the exclusion of what matters to others. Being in first position reduces your ability to understand others. You rely on your perceptions of another in your engagement. This may or may not be accurate.

Someone who spends most of their time in first position is generally seen as egotistical or insensitive.

Second position

Second position is essential in building and maintaining relationships. It represents empathy, 'putting yourself in another's shoes'. From second position, you understand how someone else experiences the world and how they experience you. You check your assumptions about what the person is thinking and feeling.

From second position you use language that refers things to the other person, for example, 'I notice you are... ', 'I hear you say... ', 'That seems to suggest you are... ', 'I don't know if this is right, but you seem... '.

Operating predominately in second position means that you spend too much time paying attention to others and you may lose your self.

Someone stuck in second position is generally seen as a caretaker or rescuer.

Third position

From third position you experience the situation as an external, neutral observer – even if you are a participant. You watch what happens. You understand it without experiencing the direct emotions of those involved (including yourself).

In third position you use language that is impersonal, such as 'It seems that…', 'We might assume…', 'People sometimes…'.

Operating predominately in third position means that you develop only superficial relationships.

You lose your own sense of self.

Someone stuck in third position is generally seen as detached, impersonal and cold.

Imagine if someone shouts at you or is angry with you. If you respond in first position you take it personally. You respond with your emotions and may feel overwhelmed or shout back. Either is unlikely to be the best response. First position is the least helpful to manage relational or emotional situations.

If you respond in second position you are likely to notice the other's anger or distress. Locating the emotion in them helps you to avoid reacting to it. You maintain your calm and engage without matching the emotion. You might respond by naming the anger. You might suggest ways to have a discussion to resolve the issue. Second position is the most helpful position in this instance.

If you respond in third position, you are likely to observe the emotion. You will comment on the dynamics of your interaction. You may say something like 'It seems that you are quite upset with this. Each time we raise this issue, it seems to end up in an emotional shouting match. What do we need to change?' Taking this position will be most helpful if it follows a response that creates empathy.

Shifting between thinking positions

Robyn shared responsibility for a transformational change program in a large global organisation. She was then new to the organisation. Everything was new: the owners, the CEO and her relationship with her joint project owner. The change process was described by stakeholders as 'undoable': what a challenging situation!

Robyn felt herself becoming stuck fixing operational crises. She knew that this was not high value work for a C-suite executive. There was a lack of capability in critical areas of need in the organisation. She felt responsible for making sure they got them right.

Imagining the perspective of the joint change owner enabled a profound shift in Robyn's thinking. It enabled her to shift from what was happening to her, to what her colleague's experience might be like. Her compassion increased visibly as she reflected on this. She tuned into cues from earlier conversations and realised her colleague felt out of his depth. The colleague knew he wasn't the first choice for the role. He was not spending enough time with his young daughter. He was open with Robyn in questioning whether he wanted to continue in the role.

As they were joint project owners, they shared success and failure. They could only succeed if they united, which they hadn't. Robyn identified some tactics for engaging together. She suggested joint daily 'triage' meetings to deal with all project issues and keep them on top of what was happening. That would allow them to be more proactive and less reactive. This would also serve the important purpose of becoming a united front. A united front to their teams and the organisation would likely minimise some of the issues.

This shift in thinking, from first into second and then third, was invaluable in unsticking the problems. With the shift,

Robyn physically relaxed; her shoulders relaxed. She was able to identify constructive actions that would improve her relationships during her working day, and her relationship with her colleague.

Managing attention

Overall, your attention is divided amongst the three positions.

Being aware of how you control your attention allows you to organise it to achieve the outcomes you seek.

As a leader, first position should receive the least amount of your attention – about 15% – as you focus less on you. Your job is to get the work done through others. About half of your attention is focused in second position. This allows you to monitor the people with whom you relate and to deal with issues as they arise. About 35% of your attention is in third position. You need to maintain perspective on the interactions around you, to manage ideas and information and to manage the situation.

When you are actively coaching, you may find that second position takes a greater percentage of your attention – maybe as high as 75% – with first position back to 5% to 10%, and third at about 10% to 15%.

Activity

1. Consider how much of your time you spend in each of first, second and third positions. Where do you spend most of your time?

2. How flexibly do you move between these three positions?
3. How might you increase the time you spend in second position, so that it is about 50% of your time?
4. Consider your team members. How do you believe they spend their time?
5. What might you be able to do to help them increase their flexibility?

How unhooking your thinking helps you to coach

It's quite easy for our thoughts to hook us. We can become stuck in our thinking. We can't rid our minds of a particular thought. We are not able to make change or take action that we know will be usefu; instead we get caught up in a negative loop. That was the case of Robyn, above.

Team members are the same. There will be times when you can see that their thinking is stuck. They are hooked on a thought or belief that is unhelpful for them. This is very normal. It's pretty much what all minds do. Our minds judge, compare and tend to predict the worst.

When this happens, our thinking is fused. It becomes a problem when the feeling of being stuck evokes a negative reaction. These are the hooks that hold back change: it's the inner voice telling us, 'I'm not good enough', 'I'll fail', 'Nobody likes me', 'I'll look foolish', 'I don't deserve it'. Instead of being thoughts that *we have*, our thoughts *have us*[26]. We are hooked.

The thoughts that have you

As coach, it can be helpful to identify the 'thoughts that have you'. These hooks affect how we talk about ourselves. They become fused with our identity and the stories we tell about ourselves. They become a boundary that may have protected us in the past but now they prevent our growth.

Recognising your own hooks

Anna, a highly accomplished young leader, as her current goal chose to liberate herself from her internal voices. She wanted to be able to hear her 'own self'.

She replayed conflicting parental voices. One was a highly critical 'you will never be any good', and the other was 'take risks, strive hard, achieve'. The internal conflict reflected her current impasse and helped to liberate herself from it. For her, these internal voices were quite intrusive. Coaching allowed her to transform her confusion and discomfort into a catalyst for her growth. Having made progress here, she was able to focus on the career and other leadership goals that brought her to coaching.

For others, recognising that such thoughts are happening is enough. Bringing patterns to the surface to identify specific criticisms opens them up to examination.

What's important is how workable your thoughts are for you. Respond to your inner thoughts and criticisms in terms of their workability (how helpful they are) rather than worry about how true they are.

As uncomfortable as it is, clarifying and examining critical internal voices allows us to make choices about their value. Then we can shift the level of influence they have over us.

Managing your inner voices

John identified that his 'you idiot, why don't you see the world as I do' inner voice led during difficult conversations to an overwhelming anger. He described this experience as a 'red mist descending'. He was pretty horrified at himself for the emotional outbursts that followed. Yet he felt trapped into them. Practising an acceptance mindfulness technique unhooked him from his negative thoughts and feelings. He could stop fighting against them and experience them less.

Using humour, reframing and exploring the workability are other useful techniques to quieten your negative thoughts.

When you feel hooked or pulled, and a negative emotion results, take a pause. Note the feeling. What triggered it? What did your mind say or do that hooked you? How did your behaviour change when you were hooked? Did you manage to unhook yourself? How?

Experiment with noticing these feelings, recording them and reflecting on your observations. The activity below provides a frame for doing this. Once you have noticed a pattern, consider how you might increase your cognitive flexibility. Use the techniques suggested elsewhere in this chapter.

As coach, you can also help your team members unhook from limiting self-beliefs and doubts.

Activity

Record instances where you feel hooked. Use the prompts below to guide what you notice. Notice any patterns.

- What's the trigger?
- What did your mind say or do to hook you?
- How did your behaviour change when you got hooked?
- What did those actions cost you?
- Did you manage to unhook yourself? If so, how?

Example 1:

- **What's the trigger?** Meeting with XXX. XXX GMs were listing all reasons why it was difficult to do, would take too long, was very complex, no point in doing it, etc. I had anticipated there would be technical resistance, so had invited a finance leader who knew the systems and processes well to help build a roadmap.
- **What did your mind say or do to hook you?** When they started with the objections around why it shouldn't or couldn't be done, my first reaction was, 'I am not surprised'. I started well with saying they are the stakeholders and my role was to facilitate the process. When they kept getting bogged down, my first reaction was, 'typical XXX mindset'.
- **How did your behaviour change when you got hooked? What did those actions cost you?** I started to become impatient and said, 'Let's talk more about the "how" rather than the "why"; other organisations are able to create this visibility so why not us?' I could see them getting defensive and digging their heels in.

- **Did you manage to unhook yourself? If so, how?** Yes, I did. I asked the supportive XXX person for their input and ensured we were all ready to listen. She elaborated a potential roadmap to build what we wanted. Once others heard from 'one of them' they were more engaged and committed to getting the work done.

Example 2:

- **What's the trigger?** Leadership team meeting to understand how we could improve the data accuracy and completeness in the global system. One of the members suggested hiring a team of data analysts to cleanse the data.
- **What did your mind say or do to hook you?** Here we go again, no accountability or ownership of business data. How could an external team resolve our core data without business knowledge? How many times do we need to go through this? Why is it so hard to understand?
- **How did your behaviour change when you got hooked? What did those actions cost you?** My frustration would have been evident in my voice and the logical points I rattled off in response to the suggestion. XXX attended the meeting and walked away with the view that I don't listen, don't make allowances for lack of knowledge/experience in others.
- **Did you manage to unhook yourself? If so, how?** I did not manage to unhook myself in this instance. When XXX shared her opinion of my behaviour at that meeting, I called up the person who made the suggestion to apologise. I learnt that sometimes it does take considerable time to get people on the same page and it can't be rushed.

Example 3:

- **What's the trigger?** Lack of buy-in, taking too much time to agree with me, resistance.
- **What did your mind say or do to hook you?** Progress is slow, and I have to push through to make it happen. It's frustrating!
- **How did your behaviour change when you got hooked? What did those actions cost you?** I talked over everyone, became impatient, lost sight of my goal.
- **Did you manage to unhook yourself? If so, how?** Lots of deep breaths before and during meetings. Having someone supportive in the meeting. Changing my perspective – how do I help them play their role as leaders consistently?

How to be less biased

Sometimes it feels hard enough to work on the hooks and cognitive challenges we know we have. But there are others that we remain unaware of. Decisions are often driven by thoughts and feelings of which we are unaware. Yet they profoundly influence the way we engage and with whom.

As coach, you need to become more aware of when unconscious beliefs might limit how you engage with particular individuals. That way you can mitigate against the beliefs.

It is possible to miminise the negative influence unconscious thinking has on decisions – including decisions on who we coach, how we coach them and how much effort we put into coaching them.

Our minds are like icebergs. A small but powerful fraction of our thinking is available to our conscious minds (the tip of the iceberg). Despite popular belief, most of our decisions aren't made at the conscious level through rational, logical processes. It's estimated that our unconscious mind deals with between 8 million and 40 million pieces of information in a second. In that same second, our conscious mind is capable of dealing with only about 40. Our unconscious mind handles all this information by taking a number of shortcuts, relying on patterns that have become so well learned they are automatic. This significantly helps our decision making. We don't have to go into the same situation 50 times and experience it as brand new each time we do[31].

When we encounter a person, group, or an issue we are familiar with, the shortcut pops into mind within a split second. For example, we see an individual, notice her gender, and the category of 'women' is activated. Once activated, the associations are difficult to inhibit or suppress. The activated belief is likely to drive subsequent behaviour, judgments and decisions[32].

The bad news is that the shortcuts may create bias and distortion. By categorising individuals as members of groups we minimise their individuality. This shuts down a host of valuable information, leading to misjudgments. We apply group characteristics, whether or not they apply to particular individuals; for example, women put family first and career second.

It is common to hold contradictory sets of beliefs. It is common to express conscious beliefs that contradict unconscious beliefs on contentious issues. We express support for women in leadership roles, yet hold beliefs that women's primary responsibility is family. In general, what we say represents conscious beliefs, while what we do represents unconscious beliefs.

Weigh up the costs and benefits

Conscious associations shape responses where people have the opportunity to weigh up costs and benefits.

Unconscious associations influence responses that are more difficult to control. These include non-verbal responses, or responses that are automatic that people don't try to 'control'. Unconscious beliefs influence most when:

- We don't have clear decision making criteria;
- We don't have or take the time to deliberate on our decisions;
- Information is ambiguous so it's not clear how it helps us make the decision; and
- There is no open scrutiny of the decision.

Under these circumstances, our decision making may be biased.

The following are biases that occur when unconscious beliefs influence decision making[33]:

- **Affinity bias:** We like people who are most like us, those with whom we share an affinity such as gender, culture or style, and we favour them over others. To what extent might affinity bias who you coach?
- **Expectancy bias:** We create expectations and interpret others' behaviour using people categories. Professor Nalini Joshi avoids wearing a black suit to a business

function. She is often mistaken for wait staff, despite being one of Australia's foremost mathematics scholars[34]. In a largely white culture, we expect a woman with brown skin to be in a support/service role rather than the keynote speaker. How do your associations influence the expectations you have of people from different cultures?

- **Confirmation bias:** We pay attention to behaviour that confirms people categories. We disregard information that disconfirms it. We may pay attention when women appear unconfident but disregard it when women appear confident. We seek out information that confirms our stereotypes and ignore or reinterpret it when it does not.
- **Directive bias:** We use gender schema to direct the context so that gender-consistent information is elicited. For example, we are more likely to ask women about their children, and men about their work. Conversations at work with women about their families reinforce their role in child-rearing. We may ask someone who does not have white skin where they were born and be embarrassed when they answer 'Australia' with a broad Aussie twang. How much might this affect the choices you make when you coach?
- **Self-selection bias:** Women's own biases cause them to opt out of opportunities. For example, women may apply harsher judgment about their suitability for promotion. As coach, what might you do to help them to more accurately assess their capabilities?

Here are five strategies you can employ to make better decisions:

1. **Slow down and focus your attention.** Associations are more likely to come into play when decisions are made quickly and intuitively. Be mindfully present and aware when you are making decisions about your team members. Take the time to consider a variety of options, weighing the costs and benefits of each.
2. **Cultivate empathy and connection.** Focus first on relationship, then on task.
3. **Question yourself.** Question your motives, assumptions and choices. What's another way to see this? What further information do you need? What assumptions are you making? What assumptions can you see this person making that limit their choices?
4. **Review multiple perspectives.** Take a broader frame of reference, discuss options with people who think differently to you. How do others see this? Try some 'What if' scenarios. Take the opposite perspective and ask 'Why not'?
5. **Commit to action.** Identify what gets in your way of fair thinking. Keep focused on improving yourself.

Activity

1. Think about your next coaching session with someone who represents a different demographic to you. How might you use the above strategies?
2. How will you ensure that your interaction is not rushed, and that you are mindfully present for that person?
3. Review multiple perspectives and help the person being coached to do the same. How might you ensure a range of perspectives will be considered?

Shape new perspectives by creating distinctions

When coaches create distinctions for coachees, it helps them to see things in new ways. Using the multiple perspectives that coaches bring, new ways of seeing things and conclusions can be explored.

Making distinctions is like using a telescope: each change of your lens lets you see things quite differently. When you focus close-up, you don't notice what is far away. When you look into the distance, the foreground becomes invisible.

One of the premises in coaching is that it enables people to grow and develop. They can move readily towards want they want to achieve and who they want to be. Coaching aims to clarify assumptions and how they help or interfere with goal-directed behaviour and growth.

We all make particular assumptions and have different ways of seeing the world. We may or may not be aware of them or even be able to articulate them all. Even so, they will affect our choices: we pay attention to certain things, yet miss others. We take certain actions, but not others.

To help people to take new actions, coaches need to assist them to flex their assumptions.

Have you heard about the invisible gorilla test[35]? If you have not, follow the link in the references and watch the video. It shows how much we can miss of what goes on around us. Something may be right in front of our eyes, yet we don't notice it because of our assumptions.

In opening people up to their assumptions, the purpose is to first make them aware of what the assumptions are. Second, it broadens the choice of opportunities that exist. Also, it brings conscious and unconscious choices into clearer alignment.

Making distinctions helps to do this.

Distinctions help us to see things in different ways, to gain insight and to expand our horizons.

To make a distinction means to draw attention to other ways to see a 'fact' or 'idea'.

When we introduce alternatives, we often rely on an argumentative stance, such as 'You're wrong', 'Look at it my way', which is rarely effective. Making distinctions is less confrontational. It offers new suggestions that will interest or intrigue an open mind. Here are some ways to go about it.

Use different language

Switching the language you use can be a way of uncovering assumptions. Play back to people the *particular words and expressions* they use. This can help them to notice the assumption that sits behind the words. Replacing their word with another that contradicts it draws their attention to it. For example, 'You've stated X as a problem. What are the opportunities to learn here?' Highlighting the 'problem' helps to assess why it is a problem and to open up the opportunity to ask whether it is a problem. The word 'learn' helps to reframe the discussion.

Or, 'You've said this can't be done. What if you could do it?' You are inviting the person to explore the opposite of what they can imagine.

Use storytelling

Using a story, metaphor or simile to speak about the 'issue' less directly allows existing connections to be questioned. You can then notice different connections. For example, I used the lens and telescope analogy earlier in this section.

If someone tells you about what seems to be a potential crisis situation, yet they do not seem to be proactively responding to it, you might say to them, 'Your issue is like a bomb about to go off. What would your first steps be to disarm it?' This distinction draws a different level of awareness to the situation.

> **Example:** Ray described her team member Dan's behaviour as like a sandstorm obscuring the foundation. Ray knew that Dan had the skills to engage with senior stakeholders. But in the current project he wasn't engaging them often enough, or with enough authority. The metaphor galvanised Dan's thinking and helped him to focus on the sandstorm. The conversation then turned to the lack of confidence that Dan offered as the heart of the issue. 'The sandstorm' became the substance of the conversation, rather than how to change or manage the stakeholders.

Flexibly position your thinking

We discussed this in the previous chapter. It involves taking specific positions from which to see the issue.

> **Activity**
>
> When you are coaching, make sure you are fully present and paying close attention to the words and the expressions that are used. Then use distinctions.

1. Prepare for coaching by reflecting on habitual language and turns of phrase that the person uses. Explore some alternatives. Try finding opposites; use a thesaurus to find alternative words if that helps. What are some options to focus on?
2. How would you ask for a distinction in the coaching conversation? Plan the questions you could use.
3. Identify some metaphors. What are the person's hobbies or interests? How could you use their own interests as a lens for exploring their working world differently? For example, if they enjoy gardening or sailing, think of some metaphors that you might make use of.

7

Warm it up like a coach

You've worked on your presence, your power, trust and cognitive flexibility. Now you're ready for the pre-game warm-up. This chapter focuses on some basics that will help you in any coaching conversation. It also helps you to focus on how you create opportunities to coach.

Coaching basics

The four coaching basics support coaching conversations, no matter their purpose: whether they are everyday, business-as-usual or feedback conversations or even challenging conversations. The coaching basics are:

1. Create psychological safety
2. Develop rapport so that you are in sync with the coachee
3. Listen actively to them
4. Ask open questions to expand the conversation and maintain the coaching purpose.

When you learn to juggle, it can be hard work to get all the balls moving to the right rhythm and to keep them all in the air.

It's helpful to start with one ball, then add the second, mastering each step one at a time. Starting off with the whole task is too daunting. You wouldn't just throw all the balls in the air and hope to start juggling! Learning to have new kinds of conversations is the same.

Example: When Marlena was developing herself to coach more, she found that she would freeze up a little. When she was about to begin a coaching conversation where she wanted to try out her new skills, she was overthinking it. She was trying to assemble everything she had learned, to be fully prepped. She reminded herself that her basics were the same even though her conversations had different purposes.

Why psychological safety matters to coaching

Psychological safety provides a strong foundation for a great coaching relationship. When leaders actively pay attention to psychological safety they set up a context that allows team members to bring their full selves in.

"Psychological safety describes perceptions of the consequences of taking interpersonal risks in a particular context... it facilitates the willing contribution of ideas and actions to a shared enterprise."[36]

Being fully present in a team can be challenging for some team members. Wisely, people won't risk the challenge of swinging out on the trapeze if there isn't a safety net. Likewise, in teamwork, they won't risk the challenge of bringing their full selves in if there isn't the right level of psychological safety. Your job as the coach is to create the safety net and maintain it in good order.

How to create psychological safety

For people to feel safe at work you need to meet five important human needs:

1. I matter. My being here has value.
2. I belong. I feel like I am a part of this team.
3. I'm enabled. I have what I need to contribute to the team.
4. I contribute. What I do makes a difference to the team.
5. I'm respected. You recognise me for who I am.

Establishing a set of ground rules can help you to pay explicit attention to these needs and you can involve your team in the process.

Psychological safety creates a climate that increases the chances of learning behaviour.

It supports people to engage in collaborative work and undertake new activities. They are more likely to seek help, experiment and discuss errors or mistakes. This climate is a strong foundation for coaching.

Psychological safety also increases as people share more personal information about who they are. Team-building and social activities help people get to know more about each other. Personal sharing activities in a strong safety context will help you to meet the human needs listed above.

Specific tactics that you can use as part of the coaching process which will increase psychological safety are:

- Use your coach presence and be vulnerable to make authentic connections with your team

- Provide protection and support when team members encounter difficulty or challenges
- Promote feedback as a two-way opportunity for professional growth for both team members and yourself (and see the section on feedforward in Chapter 9)
- Provide support for overcoming adversity: help to reframe problems and identify strengths from which to leverage
- Encourage people to share diverse interests and perspectives.

Activity

1. How would you rate the level of psychological safety in your team?

   Very low — Quite low — Average — Quite high — Very high

2. Is psychological safety present for all your team members? Who are the individuals that you need to pay particular attention to, to ensure the level of safety is right for them?
3. How do you establish psychological safety as you begin coaching individuals?
4. How well do people in your team know each other? What information do you share about yourself? How do you encourage team members to share personal information about themselves?
5. How much do you encourage the expression of diverse interests and perspectives?
6. How readily do people tend to present alternative views to yours, build on your views or disagree with you?

7. What's one thing you could do immediately to increase psychological safety for your team?

Getting in sync: why you should build rapport

When we are in sync with another person, we feel a positive emotional resonance with them. This connection – the sense of harmony – is rapport. Rapport is not just about the words we use and their meanings. It runs beneath the words and is unspoken. It operates on an emotional level.

As Daniel Goleman says in *The Focused Leader*, *"Rapport feels good, generating the harmonious glow of being simpatico, a sense of friendliness where each person feels the other's warmth, understanding and genuineness."*[22]

When we engage and enjoy a smooth interaction with another person, this is rapport. In existing relationships, it often begins as soon as we meet the other person. For new relationships, it may take 15 to 20 minutes of conversation for rapport to build. With some people, and some interactions, we may not achieve rapport at all, in which case the interaction feels uncomfortable. We usually attempt to finish it as soon as possible.

Figure 7.1 overleaf depicts the rapport-building process. To build rapport, and set up a good connection for your coaching you need:

- **Shared attention** – Begin with a source of mutual interest. Mutual interest helps you to focus your attention together. Two-way attention evokes shared feelings.
- **Shared feelings** encourage mutual empathy. When each person senses the other's interest in how they feel and that they are tuned into us, it feels good. This leads to...

- **Shared non-verbal behaviours.** Our actions become coordinated. The pace and timing of a conversation, matched body movements, and leaning close to each other, occur.

Then you have started to build rapport.

Figure 7.1 – The rapport-building model

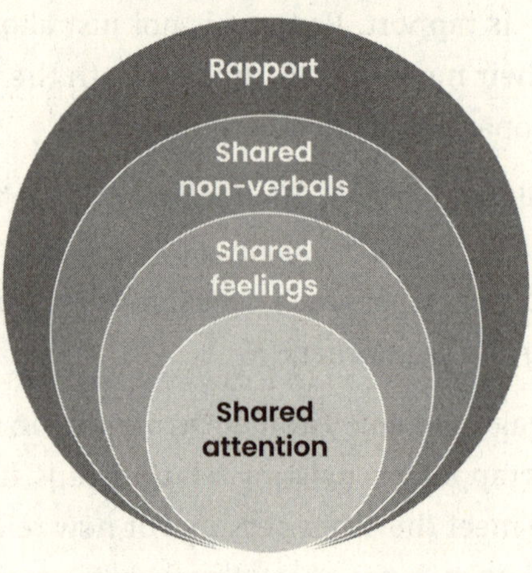

Rapport has a great deal of value for coaching. It feels good and generates a positive emotional bond. It enables you to have tougher constructive and challenging conversations. And it strengthens, not damages, the relationship. The team member may even report it as a positive interaction.

Without rapport, and where there is ill-feeling in the relationship, everything else becomes much harder. For relationships such as these, consider what you might do to build rapport and establish a better connection. Make this your priority. When you have increased rapport, then you can focus on the work.

Activity

1. Consider your team members. Which relationships have a good level of rapport, and which are lacking rapport?
2. Choose a relationship where increased rapport would have a positive impact on the relationship.
3. To increase rapport in that relationship, focus on:
   - Fostering mutual interests
   - Sharing warmth and positive feelings
   - Being responsive to and mirroring non-verbal cues.
4. What actions might you next take to increase rapport in this relationship?

First listen. Active listening is core to coaching

Active listening is critical for good coaching. If you can't hear the other person's perspective, you can't coach. Use your empathy to put yourself in the context of the other person, really pay attention to them, then coach.

Active listening takes a stillness, a calm. In this stillness, you can take the opportunity to listen to the song beneath the words. Listening means knowing what others have said and what they meant to say. It leaves others feeling comfortable that they have had their say.

Listening begins with:

- Being patient;
- Not interrupting; and
- Listening for the underlying meaning.

Most people know how to listen. The biggest problem with listening is that leaders don't do it enough. Or they do it selectively, some of the time but not enough of the time, with some people but not others.

Even if you believe that you know what the other person is going to say, don't interrupt! If you interrupt whenever you think you know, you are likely to shut them down.

Active listening means more than not speaking. Active listening means that you show that you are paying attention. You can do this by:

- Actively checking in on your understanding;
- Asking for examples;
- Asking questions to clarify the meaning;
- Paraphrasing what you have heard; and
- Summarising to make it clear that you have listened and understood.

Avoid competitive listening, where you are most interested in finding an opening or a weak point from which to promote your own view and shoot the other one down in flames. Don't pretend to listen!

Benefits of active listening include:

- People feel heard, and sometimes that's all they're looking for;
- People are more likely to notice the flaws in their own reasoning when they hear themselves say it out loud;
- Reciprocity – if you listen carefully to me, I am more likely to listen carefully to you; and

- Identifying areas of disagreement and agreement to put them in perspective.

Activity

1. Of the people around you at work, who is a good listener? What makes them good? What do you appreciate about what they do?
2. Considering the important elements of listening, what do you think are your relative strengths and your gaps, for example:
   - I stay quiet, not speaking
   - I pay attention
   - I inquire more deeply
   - I check for understanding
   - I show that I have understood.
3. Choose one person who you feel you should listen more carefully to. How will you make sure you listen to them more carefully next time you have the opportunity to do so?

How open questions expand coaching conversations

Questions that expand thinking and open lines of inquiry are a key tool for good coaching.

Example: Alex says that she had to stop herself and think carefully when she switched to a coaching style. She has had to work hard to make it a habit. It's hard to do, and she found it awkward and clunky at first. She has to shift from the usual leader habit of answering everyone's questions, to asking a question herself. It's more natural now.

Yet Alex says she still sometimes finds herself starting to answer, then stops mid-sentence, pulling herself up. She says to the other person, 'Sorry, I'm going to stop right now and ask you about that.' The feedback she receives is reinforcing for her. A new team leader said to her recently, 'Something I've noticed about you is that you never answer straight away. You make me stop and think, and I have to answer the question myself.' This is feedback that Alex is proud to receive.

Open questions allow the coachee to take ownership of the conversation's direction. They expand their thinking. Open questions prevent telling, directing, answering, knowing, all of which close off thinking.

Questions work like funnels in conversations. If you start with closed questions, you'll only get contraction. Open questions create expansion (see Figure 7.2 below).

Figure 7.2 – The effect of types of questions

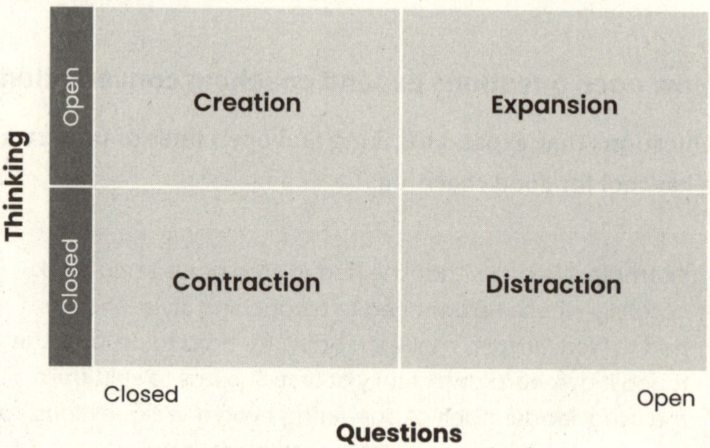

Closed and leading questions offer little opportunity for growth and development. Closed questions elicit only yes, no or maybe responses. They shut down possibilities. And once answered, another question has to be immediately asked. A succession of closed questions can feel very much like an interrogation.

Closed questions start with:

- Have...?
- Will...?
- Did...?
- Must...?

Leading questions may initially seem as if they are going to be open questions, but they are not. They end with one suggestion that requires agreement or disagreement.

Leading questions start with:

- What about doing...?
- How about trying...?
- Might you consider the possibility...?

Open questions allow the respondent the space to answer the question in their own way.

Open questions start with:

- What...?
- Where...?
- How...?
- Who...?
- When...?

'Why' is an open question, but needs judicious use, as it can lead to defensiveness. There is usually another way to ask a why question as an open question. 'Why did you...?' Might be better expressed as 'What thinking led you to that conclusion?'

Activity

1. What is the ratio of open questions you use to closed questions?
2. When do you use open questions? In what circumstances are you more likely to use open questions?
3. What effect do your open questions have on a conversation?
4. What opportunities do you have for increasing the number of open questions you ask?
5. Review the Sample Open Questions at https://karenmorley.com.au/leadlikeacoach. Identify two or three questions that you would like to add to your question repertoire.

PART III

Coach

8

Play it like a coach

If you've been experimenting with and mastering the tactics outlined in the preceding chapters, you are already coaching.

The starting point for this chapter is to introduce coaching moments you can incorporate into your daily routine. These are opportunities to coach anytime, anywhere.

Most of the chapter then focuses on a specific method for having structured coaching conversations. These conversations follow a different structure to the usual task-focused meeting or performance discussions. If you are already familiar with the GROW model[37], or your organisation promotes the GROW structure, use that instead. The two models are very similar.

Create your own cadence of coaching by using a mix of coaching in the moment and extended coaching conversations to develop and support your team.

The chapter wraps up with a reminder to keep focused on your own learning, by debriefing your coaching conversations.

Create coaching moments

Don't use a coaching approach with your team members solely for performance management or in structured meetings. Provide micro-coaching in everyday 'moments'.

Used in this way, coaching has the spontaneity of a jazz band. In a jazz band, when the musicians become attuned to each other and to the moment, they adapt and respond in their playing, and call and answer as the mood takes them. The music can take many iterations, rather than rely on one predetermined score.

One of the impediments to managers using coaching more is that they claim they 'don't have the time'. I challenge this thinking because it contains within it a fundamental misconception of what it means to be a leader. What is the role of the leader? Is it to 'do'? Or is it to support others to do? The primary responsibility of leaders is to get the work done through others.

Coaching is most potent, *and* easiest to do, in day-to-day conversations.

A coaching style changes the nature of conversations. By focusing at the level of conversation, coaching is simpler and easier.

A masterclass in coaching

In 'The African Queen' Katharine Hepburn plays the prim and proper missionary. Humphrey Bogart is the hard-drinking river trader. In his article, *Coaching conversations*, Carr[38] highlights a wonderful coaching conversation in the 'twisted like a corkscrew' scene in the movie. This is when the African

Queen survives going over rapids and a waterfall, but not without suffering some damage. Hauled up on the shore, Bogart surveys the damage. A blade has broken off the boat's propeller and the shaft is twisted 'like a corkscrew'. For Bogart, that's it. Hepburn asks him what needs to be done. Bogart explains how, with the right kit, in the right port, it could all be fixed. Out here in the jungle, he sees that there's no hope.

Hepburn listens and watches. And then she gives a masterclass in coaching in the moment. She focuses Bogart's mind away from what's not possible towards what is possible. They discover a solution, repair the boat and continue their journey.

On the first level, this demonstrates the power of coaching to deal with the problems we face right now. On a deeper level, it shows how to deal with problems in general. There will always be rapids and waterfalls that we can't prepare for, or don't pay attention to. But as Hepburn shows, it is possible to confront challenges if we keep exploring options. If we stay positive and believe that there is a solution to every problem we will find it[38].

Be open to coaching conversations at any time

Coaching conversations can occur at any time. Leaders should be attuned to openings for exploring development. One of the openings you create when you focus on creating coaching moments is for development. Unless you're in a crisis, there is always time to focus on development.

For example, if your team member approaches you and asks you a question, you are most likely to answer with a solution. Rather than jumping straight to that solution, try pausing. Whether or not you know the answer becomes immaterial (at least for this conversation!).

Instead ask questions. What have you already done? What have you thought of but haven't yet tried? What information do you need to be able to answer the question yourself? What have you already tried? How did that work? What would X do in this situation? What would you do if you had different resources? What have you thought of doing next? Who else is involved?

These questions elicit more information about the context. They can help clarify what the options are, and they can help to identify new options. They can help to shape what will work and what might not work.

It's asking questions, and the questions we ask, that makes the difference.

Rather than view coaching as something to do from time to time, see it as less of a prescription. Leaders should ask themselves in every moment, not whether or not to coach, but *what to coach for*.

Activity

1. Prime yourself at the beginning of each day. Take three minutes and quickly flick through your 'to-do' list, or your calendar. Make a note of who you will be seeing. Make a note of your available time. Who might you be walking with from one meeting to the next? Who will you not be seeing, but have some feedback for? Then identify the potential coaching moments:
    - Opportunity with Person A – when, where, what
    - Opportunity at Time A – when, where, what
2. How will you ensure that you see, and seize, the moment?
3. How might you prime yourself to pause before offering solutions?

4. What might be your challenges in pausing?
5. How will you respond so that you help team members to work on identifying the solution?
6. What might be the advantages in doing this?
7. What questions will you use?

A coaching gameplan

A simple four-stage process helps to structure a quality coaching conversation[39].

The coaching circle (see Figure 8.1) is a four-stage process for a meaningful coaching conversation. You will need around 60 to 75 minutes to complete one circle.

Figure 8.1 – The coaching circle

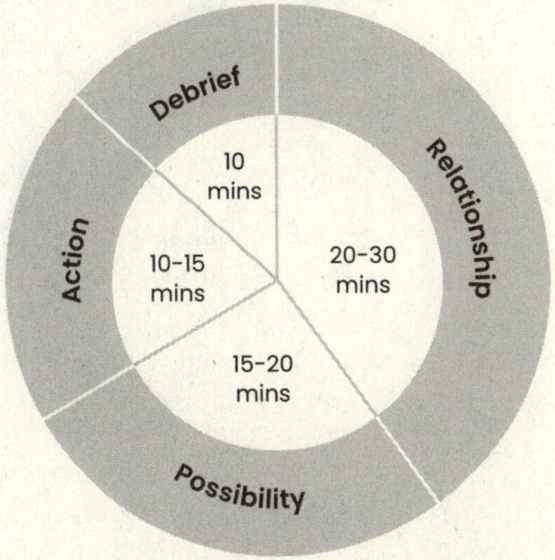

The first stage in the coaching circle is building the relationship with a coachee. This is the longest and most important circle stage.

The second stage, possibility, aims to generate many possible options – not just the first option that comes to mind, but as many options as possible, the more the better.

Having explored a variety of options, in the third stage action focuses on deciding what you will do. What will be done, by whom, by when and with what resources?

The final stage debriefs the learning. As coach you have the opportunity to reflect on your learning as you use this coaching conversation structure. As you become more proficient, you can engage your coachee to take part with you in the debrief (we cover this later in the chapter).

Start with building the relationship

Figure 8.2 – Stage 1: Relationship

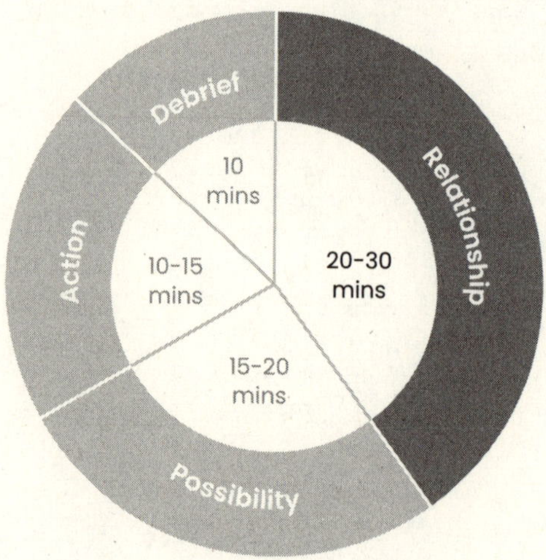

The circle process is a prescription for a successful coaching conversation. Building a relationship is the first step of the regime. Allocate about 20 to 30 minutes for this stage.

Building a relationship is an investment in the development and future performance of your coachee.

Use your coach presence that we talked about in Chapter 4. Use the coaching basics we've talked about already too. Spend time building rapport, inquiring and exploring the world of your coachee.

Do this to deeply understand the coachee, their context, their expectations and their actions. The key tool in this stage is the ability to ask open questions. The main challenge is to have the patience to avoid jumping to a solution.

How do you get started? What's the focus for the conversation? You may generate the topic for coaching or the coachee may. Maybe you start off with an explicit agenda to coach. In this first instance, you may invite the coachee to identify the issue they want coaching on.

Or perhaps in a conversation with another purpose you notice an opportunity to coach. For example, you identify a specific issue about a project or work task, or your team member might identify that they have experienced a setback. In this instance, you might pick up the thread and transition to a coaching style by saying something like, 'Let's explore what is happening and what to do here before we move on.'

If you segue into a coaching conversation, you may not have enough time to complete it. Don't rush the process, put a pause on the conversation and return to it as soon as you can. Leave it here in this stage, don't be tempted to move on to the next because your meeting time will elapse.

Or you may set up a general coaching conversation focused on development by saying, 'In our last development conversation, we set X as an objective. I'm keen to hear how you are progressing.'

What's the coachee's desired outcome? Genuine curiosity and interest in the coachee should be the basis for asking the questions. Taking the second example above to the next stage, ask, 'What, ideally, would you like to be able to do differently when we have explored what's happening?'

Use open questions to:

- Show mutual trust and respect
- Understand the person's intent
- Clarify the issue and its context
- Identify decision criteria
- Probe and challenge assumptions
- Explore feelings, attitudes, beliefs
- Offer support.

While open questions are the key tool to use here, there are others that have good value:

- Use silence, leaving time for the coachee to hear his or her own views, and to think through issues
- Use non-verbal gestures such as looking curious or thoughtful
- Prompt for more information, such as 'Tell me more about that'.

This is the part of the circle likely to be the most challenging; it may seem like it is taking too long. Stay patient and work with the process.

Activity

Create your own 'go-to' set of questions, using the Open Questions resource sheet at https://karenmorley.com.au/leadlikeacoach. The basis for asking the questions should be a genuine curiosity and interest in the coachee.

1. What questions might you use to clarify the issue and context?
2. What questions could you use to probe for or challenge the assumptions that the coachee is making?
3. What distinctions might you use to highlight issues and assumptions?
4. What questions would help you to explore feelings, attitudes and beliefs?
5. What gets in the way of you asking more open questions?

Fully explore 'lines of questions'

Coaching focuses on making a high-quality experience for the person being coached. One tactic for doing this is to stay with 'lines of questions'. As coach, make sure you explore each line of questioning, taking it to its conclusion. Avoid asking random questions based on momentary thoughts or your own interests.

Following question lines is like a flock of geese flying in formation. Each one notices the position of the other and uses their updraft/downdraft to fly in formation. As coach, each question you ask or response you make should align with the direction the coachee has taken.

While geese make this look effortless, it's not so easy in conversations. You will need to put aside your ego and your interests and listen carefully. Ask yourself, 'Have I fully explored point X, or is there further information I can elicit?' 'In what direction is this conversation going?' 'Are we moving in a particular direction to develop a deeper understanding?' 'When is it time to shift attention to another thread?'

As you keep the line of questions in mind, be aware of when the coachee sets up their own diversions. Is the openness unfamiliar or too challenging? Perhaps they don't know the answer or are distracted. While the focus is on them, and the question line is theirs, make sure they too stick with it as makes best sense.

Remember:

- Pay attention to the coachee by minimising the distractions in your head
- Listen to the answers from your coachee
- Think about the follow-up question to their response
- Follow a thread until it reaches its conclusion.

Activity

1. What is most challenging for you as you pay attention to the lines of questions?
2. What do you need to change, to better follow the lines of questions?
3. How do you sense when a line of questions finishes?

Explore possibilities to open up new options for action

Figure 8.3 – Stage 2: Possibility

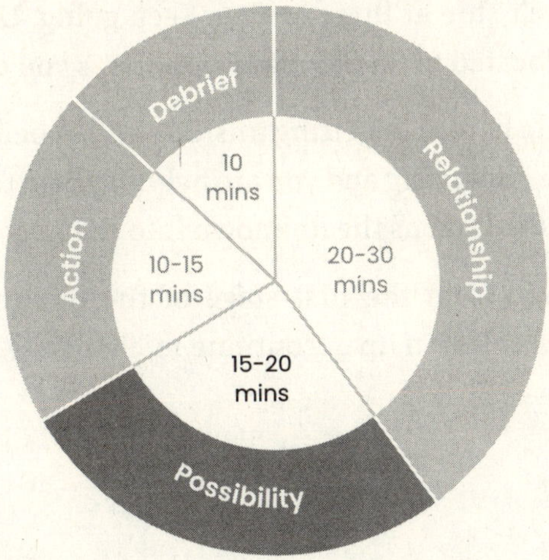

The second stage in the gameplan is to explore possibilities to open up new options for action. Allocate 15 to 20 minutes for this stage.

Your job as coach is to help the coachee to identify new possibilities, to stimulate new ideas, to offer distinctions and explore and assess a wide range of options.

The basis for your questions here is a genuine curiosity and interest in finding and exploring new options. Use open questions to generate:

- New perspectives on the situation
- Novel ideas
- Multiple options about what is possible.

There are always many more options available for action than one person can think up. Even if you feel stuck, this step is critical to help you identify them. Don't limit the number of options. Don't stop at three or five. Keep going. Use the time you have allocated to find as many options as you can.

The key value here is in getting unstuck and in being creative. The coachee is learning and you are helping them to see things not yet known. It turns the unknown into the knowable.

The challenge from the first stage of the process, to avoid jumping to a solution, may continue to challenge you during this stage.

Activity

1. Create your own 'go-to' set of questions that focus on possibility. What questions might you use to find new perspectives on the problem?
2. How might you identify and create novel ideas?
3. How will you ensure you generate multiple options? What will help you avoid stopping at the first one or two you identify?
4. How do you think you might weave some distinctions into this part of the process to help generate new ideas?
5. What do you find most challenging about this part of the process?

Turn possibilities into action

A coaching conversation needs to end in a clear commitment to action.

Coaching is not just talk, it's action.

In the third stage, allocate 10 to 15 minutes to summarise insights from the conversation and consider action steps. After exploring many options, it's important to decide what to do. Make sure that there's a clear decision for action.

Figure 8.4 – Stage 3: Action

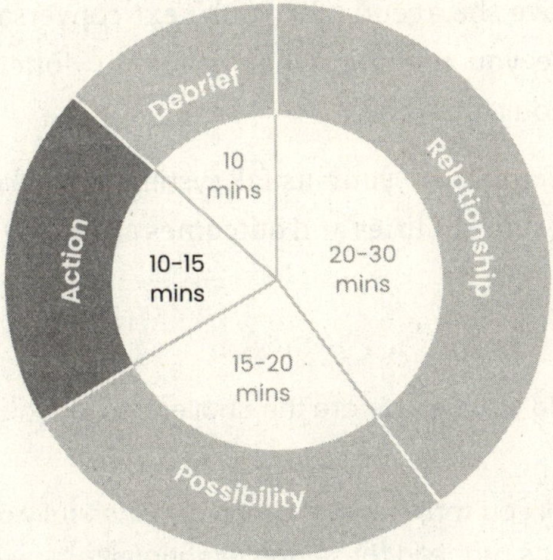

Commit to actions and timelines by:

- helping the coachee make choices about actions;
- securing commitment to the next steps;
- exploring what could go wrong and planning to avoid likely problems;
- ensuring the coachee has the right levels of support; and
- identifying how you will support them.

This is the area in which leaders feel most comfortable, when they have their manager cap on. It is the area that good coaches may pay less attention to. They may focus too much on future growth and not enough on present performance.

Without this stage, you are not having the complete coaching conversation. It moves coaching from a warm friendly conversation to being action-oriented. This is where you generate the forward movement. You gain clarity and certainty where before there was little. You are making a commitment to progress. You have the agenda for your next conversation. What progress are you making, what have you done differently, what have you achieved?

Use SMART goals or your usual system to make sure that activities, responsibilities and outcomes are all crystal clear.

Activity

1. What do you believe are the challenges for you in this stage?
2. How will you make sure that the coachee fully owns the decisions made in these conversations?
3. What commitment might you make to support the coachee to achieve his/her next steps?
4. How will you make sure you don't revert to 'boss' mode?

Debrief your learning

This important step maximises the learning value of the coaching conversations you have. It's the fourth step in the coaching conversation cycle (see Figure 8.5).

Figure 8.5 – Stage 4: Debrief

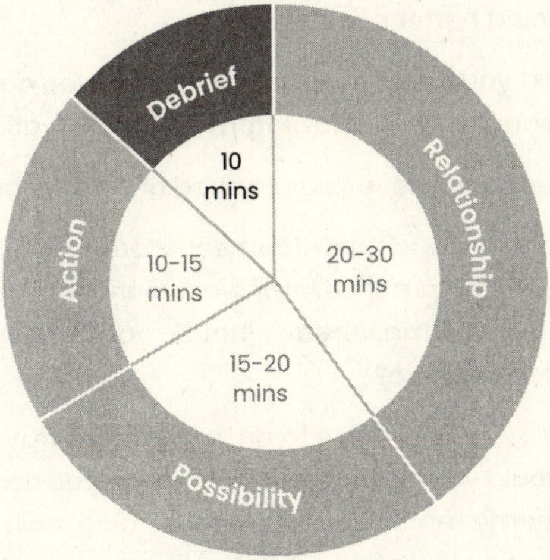

I recommend debriefing your coaching practice from time to time. Debriefing is a bit like finishing your antibiotics. You get to that time in the course of the antibiotics where you feel better, yet there are still more pills to take. You need to take the full course to get the full benefit. This process is a little like that; you get to the action stage and think you're done. But, wait, there's one more step to go.

Activity

Following your coaching conversations, capture your learning about debriefing. Chapter 9 is dedicated to feedback, which is an important part of the debrief.

You might want to return to this activity when you have read the next chapter.

1. If possible, invite the person you have been coaching to provide you with feedback. Ask one or two questions

such as: 'How helpful was the coaching for you?' 'What worked, what didn't?' 'What suggestions do you have for how I could better coach you?'

2. What did you observe about yourself as you coached? What learning do you take from your observation?
3. What feedback have you received on your coaching?
4. Refer to your coach development scoreboard. How has your coaching practice improved your coaching skills? What have you mastered? What do you need to focus on next to improve?
5. What will you undertake to do in the same way and what would you do differently next time you coach? As you become more comfortable coaching, review your progress on a monthly basis.
6. Consider how your practice is evolving. What is becoming easier to do? What have you avoided doing?
7. What's your relative balance of coaching in the moment versus coaching circle conversations? How well does the balance work for you?
8. How are your team members responding to coaching? What's changing for them? How does that make it easier or harder for you to coach them?

9

Improve the play with feedback

Feedback is a word that strikes fear into many people, so much so that we've mostly learned to avoid it. Feedback is often not given well or not offered at all. In the absence of explicit feedback on how we are going, we either keep doing what we've always done – irrespective of how effective it has been – or rely on our own feedback to ourselves. Neither is optimal for growth and development.

This chapter addresses the important and sometimes challenging areas of feedback and difficult conversations. It firstly explores why we find feedback so challenging then suggests some approaches to make it simpler and easier to give. Well-structured feedback given with the intent of improving capability is a core part of a coaching culture. The chapter then moves further into challenging territory and focuses on difficult conversations. It explains why we find certain conversations difficult and how to be more positive about them. Finally, it provides a roadmap for having a quality, if difficult, coaching conversation.

In many organisations, feedback is seldom given. So when you offer to give feedback to someone, they may become anxious, suspicious or try to avoid hearing it.

Why? Because we've mixed up a couple of simple things. We've tended to equate feedback with criticism. We see it as always about the negative, about what's wrong. And that gets in the way of good feedback, which is an important part of coaching.

When coaching, we want to focus on what to improve and what to generate. We need a way to notice where improvement is possible or needed. We need a way to notice where the gaps are and where are the opportunities for growth. As coach, your focus is always on improvement.

Regular feedback is an opportunity to improve the play.

To incorporate feedback into coaching takes courage, generativity and caring by the coach. These mindsets create a positive framework for giving feedback (see Figure 9.1). There are three especially important areas where giving regular feedback will be of great benefit:

1. **Increasing current strengths.** This is often overlooked, but it is a very powerful and positive focus for feedback. How could this person be better at what they are already good at? If someone is a great communicator with internal stakeholders, how might they grow those strengths to other areas? Are there opportunities to engage with external stakeholders?

2. **Improving current performance.** This is not a 'performance conversation'! This is an opportunity to

grow, to tweak the edges, to transfer skills to new contexts, to develop mastery.

3. **Developing capability needed in the future.** How might you moderate the enthusiasm this person has for getting things done to help them take a more strategic perspective? How can they develop that now in readiness for promotion into a more senior role? How can they develop capability for and demonstrate skills in preparation for moving into their next role? How might their job change in the future? What different skills might be needed?

Figure 9.1 – The positive feedback framework

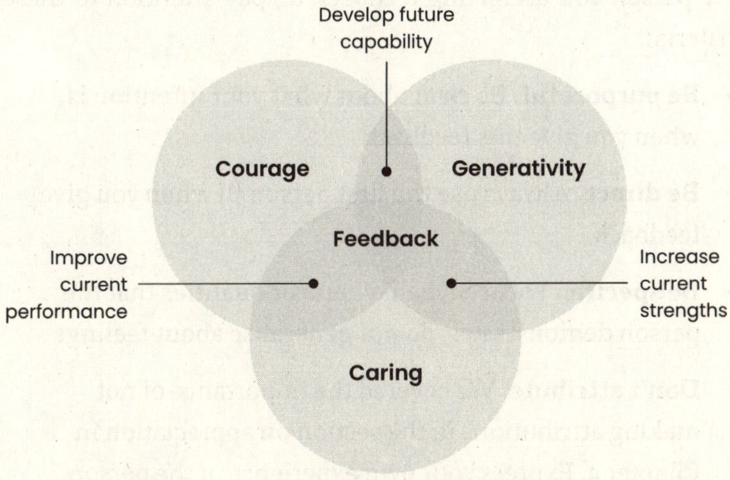

Sometimes feedback will focus on what's not working. This reshapes behaviour that is unhelpful or interferes with progress. More often feedback should focus on what's going right. This helps reinforce the right behaviour and develop mastery.

Feedback isn't criticism and criticism isn't feedback.

Most people don't give feedback, they give criticism. No wonder it doesn't go down so well!

Criticism is judgmental. It is you interpreting me – from your lens. It keeps control in the hands of the critic. It usually comes with an agenda. It's not coaching, because it reduces options rather than increases them.

Make feedback an opportunity

To turn feedback into an opportunity for both you as coach and the person you are giving feedback to, pay attention to these criteria:

- **Be purposeful.** Be clear about what your intention is when you give this feedback
- **Be direct.** Always use the first person (I) when you give feedback
- **Be specific.** Focus on behaviours or qualities that the person demonstrates, do not generalise about feelings
- **Don't attribute.** We covered the importance of not making attributions in the section on appreciation in Chapter 4. Express your own experience of the person without attempting to define who they are so the other person learns of your experience of them and their actions.

And if it isn't given first hand, it isn't feedback. If you didn't experience it, then you are giving an interpretation, not feedback. Passing feedback on is not always wise. Encourage people who come to you with 'feedback' about someone else to think about their own motives for doing so. If *they* have feedback, they should give it.

You may have heard of or even used the Situation-Behaviour-Impact (SBI) model of feedback[40]. It remains a great go-to formula for how to structure your feedback message.

In the SBI model, situation is what was observed, what happened, where, when and who was involved. Behaviour is what specifically was said or done. Impact is what difference that behaviour made to me or others around me (see Figure 9.2).

Figure 9.2 – The SBI model

Situation	Behaviour	Impact
Anchors the feedback in time, place and circumstances. Helps the receiver to understand and/ or remember the context.	Observable actions. What you would hear and see if you made a video recording. Allows the feedback receiver to know exactly what he or she did that had impact.	Feelings and thoughts the feedback giver had, and how the feedback giver or others behaved as a result of the feedback receiver's behaviour.

Below are three examples of giving feedback using the SBI approach.

Example 1: David, I noticed during this morning's presentation when you were sharing the specifics on the community partnership project, you looked above everyone's heads. I felt uncomfortable and as if you were lecturing us. I also noted that others were shifting in their seats and looking away from you.

Example 2: Carmen, when you spoke calmly and repeated what you understood me to have said, as you did in yesterday's project review, I relaxed and was able to hear your point of view. As a result we made great progress.

Example 3: Rachel, I am feeling frustrated right now because you have spoken over me several times. I am having trouble getting my point across, and don't feel heard.

If you hold in your mind the coach mindset of generativity, caring and courage, you will give valuable feedback.

Learning to give feedback is like learning to drive a car. At first the ride may be bumpy. With the courage of plenty of practice and learning from mistakes, the actions become routine, the process drops in and driving becomes automatic. Feedback likewise can become more automatic with practice.

Activity

1. What is your appetite for giving feedback?

Non-existent | Quite low | Average | Quite high | Very high

2. What experiences have contributed to this?
3. What are your barriers to giving feedback?
4. What opportunities do you think might open up if you gave more feedback?
5. Practise giving more feedback. Think of people you could give a piece of feedback to. Plan the feedback you would give to:

- **Improve current performance**: Identify the specific message for feedback, using Situation, Behaviour, Impact:

  S: ____________________

  B: ____________________

  I: ____________________

- **Increase current strengths:** Identify the specific message for feedback, using Situation, Behaviour, Impact:

  S: ____________________

  B: ____________________

  I: ____________________

- **Develop future capability:** Identify the specific message for feedback, using Situation, Behaviour, Impact:

  S: ____________________

  B: ____________________

  I: ____________________

Pay feedback forward

Marshall Goldsmith's 'feedforward' process is a great technique for leaders who want to support development. It engages others in the development process[41]. Instead of asking for feedback on what has happened in the past, the process involves asking for suggestions to improve in the future.

Feedforward flips the feedback-giving process on its head. It sets up a constructive context for increasing feedback in your team. It is a structured way to stay in charge of your feedback, make sure it's relevant and keep it constructive and helpful. It takes a lot of the heat out of getting and giving feedback.

The flip is that feedforward helps you to *"focus on the promise of the future rather than the mistakes of the past"*[41].

The idea for you as coach is to deepen your feedback culture by putting yourself first.

You can engage and encourage a feedback-ready culture by seeking feedforward.

This models to your team the value of feedback and shows that it can be helpful and positive.

Involving your stakeholders in your development process can be a powerful motivator for you, as well as highly rewarding. It is the people you work with every day who are the best 'experts' in how your behaviour could improve. The feedforward process systematically engages them in your development.

Feedforward differs from feedback in some important ways. Feedback gives you a rear-view mirror perspective on what you've already done. Its value is limited. If feedback is solely focused on your past behaviour, there isn't much that you can do about it, it's done. Sometimes feedback can seem like judgment and that can make it uncomfortable.

Feedforward is instead focused on what's ahead, the future. Feedforward is a process of asking for suggestions about future action, based on development goals. You can definitely do something about your future actions and those of your coachee.

Here's how feedforward works in practice:

1. Set your development goals

Set your development goals and then identify between four and eight key stakeholders you would like to engage.

2. Seek suggestions for improvement

Once you have established your development goals, invite stakeholder involvement. Make your invitation to them specific, brief and positive.

Don't choose only your fans; look to get a balanced stakeholder view. Don't expect instant help or take up too much of anyone's time. Meet with or email your stakeholders with a brief outline of your goals, for example to be a better listener/ to improve your delegation.

Ask them for suggestions, such as, 'What can I do in my relationship with you to demonstrate better listening/better delegation? Give me one or two suggestions that I can work on in the next month.'

Now is not the time for procrastination! Don't wait for a better time to ask. Keep your emotional tone calm and steady; avoid seeming to be sceptical or doubtful. And don't put yourself down as you ask!

Listen actively to the responses given to you. Give the person your undivided attention as you are asking for their suggestions and record what they say. Clarify what you heard them say. Don't try to explain your behaviour, make excuses or appear annoyed at what they are telling you.

At the end of the conversation, thank them: 'Thank you for your suggestions. I will think this over and respond to you via email within the next week.' Don't be insincere, artificial or appear dejected.

All up, the conversation with your stakeholders should only take a couple of minutes. You don't want to engage in dialogue or debate; just stick with the facts. You don't want reams of suggestions – one or two are enough. If you think this will be challenging as a face-to-face conversation, use email.

3. Decide on your new actions

Once you have received your suggestions from your stakeholders, think about them. You may have many or you may have a few. Consider what you're doing well, what obstacles you face and what you could do differently. Assess the benefits of changing your behaviour. Avoid validating yourself or attempting to disprove the input you've received.

Choose a couple of the suggestions that you will work on. Don't overcommit and choose too many – select areas that are most likely to have the greatest impact for you. Make sure you have opportunities coming up in the next month when you can put the suggestions into play.

Draft your action plan for the month; what suggestions are you going to focus on?

Respond to your stakeholders with your action plan. Email is an efficient way to do this. Thank them first for their suggestions. Keep your email brief and simple and focused on the future. Summarise the suggestions. Don't procrastinate!

4. Act on the suggestions

Make some changes! Implement your action plan and work hard to make change visible. Don't expect instant success.

5. Review

Make sure you follow up at the end of the month. Organise your monthly stakeholder emails/meetings and follow through in a timely fashion. Keep the conversation simple, for example, 'This was my goal', 'This was the action I intended to take', 'This is what I did', 'What feedback do you have for me?'

You might need to check your ego at the door for these conversations! You also might need to push to get specifics. You need specific information about your behaviours and their impact to help you to improve. Take care not to push too hard – you want this stakeholder to stay engaged.

6. Repeat

Continue this process over a period of time. The best teams embed this practice in 'how we do things here'.

Feedforward in practice

Peter's team committed to feedforward as part of their ongoing development. They decided to incorporate the process of asking for suggestions into their monthly team meetings. To start the process, each team member outlined their development goals. Then every other team member provided them with one suggestion for improvement. Each person then decided which action they would focus on first.

At first, the process was a little stilted. This was new behaviour and it required public sharing with the team.

Peter was consistent and steadfast. He wanted the team to be high-performing, and he saw feedforward as a good way to achieve this.

He started by sharing his own goals and he set the tone when he provided suggestions to others. He kept his suggestions future-focused; he didn't yield to the temptation to provide feedback on something that had already happened. He encouraged others and he guided those who had trouble articulating their suggestions.

Over time, the team developed the habit of regular feedforward updates as part of their monthly team meetings. The team climate improved. Team members asked for and volunteered feedback more often and were more accepting of suggestions to change. As they made changes, their confidence in the process increased. Practising feedforward continued outside of the monthly team meetings and they incorporated it into daily exchanges.

The one thing that they all agreed improved was that when team members experienced adversity, they knew the others 'had their backs'. They felt they received much more support.

Activity

1. Identify key stakeholders you would like to engage in feedforward. Include as many as you feasibly can.
2. What are your focus areas? What do you need to keep in mind as you ask for suggestions?
3. What might you need to keep in mind as you listen to the suggestions?

4. Once you have received suggestions from your stakeholders, think about them. What suggestions will you focus on? Make sure you confirm with your stakeholders which ones these will be.
5. How have you organised yourself to remember to follow up in one month?
6. What have you learnt about feedback from engaging in this process?
7. How will you introduce this to your team?

Steps for giving good feedback

You can become more comfortable with the process of giving feedback if you use a clear step-by-step structure. Here is a clear map to make it easier to navigate the tough territory of feedback. This is a more defined conversation structure than that outlined earlier in Chapter 8 but keep the spirit of the coaching circle process going. Make sure that you focus on building the relationship and that you explore plenty of possibilities.

There are five key ingredients for clear feedback:

1. It has a clear business purpose
2. It is based on observation
3. It is specific
4. It is timely
5. It will improve performance.

There are seven steps in this good feedback process.

Step 1. Connect

Connect with the person on the purpose of your conversation. Ask them for permission to give feedback. Tell them why you want to give feedback and, if appropriate, ask them how they feel about receiving feedback.

Step 2. Appreciate/contextualise

Make sure you focus on what you appreciate about what the person does and acknowledge the contributions they make. This is to make sure that they see the feedback in its context – whether it's constructive feedback about something they need to improve, or something they do well and could improve further.

Step 3. Describe

Use the SBI formula from above to work through what happened and what the impact was.

Step 4. Validate

Your feedback is your perception. Inquire about what the coachee noticed about the situation and how it played out. What impact did they notice? What were they intending? What sense do they make of your feedback?

Step 5. Set goals

What change would they like to see? Share your views on the change they identify. What do you think is possible?

Step 6. Explore options

Discuss possibilities for what they could do. Ask them what responsibility they could take for change. And offer your support for their change. What will you do? What support could you offer?

Step 7. Commit to specific changes and follow through

End the conversation with confirmation on what will change and what the commitments are. How will you work together and follow through?

Activity

1. Plan a feedback coaching conversation. First, be clear on what the feedback is about. Use the SBI model to prepare it.
2. Consider what you will do to prepare, conduct and follow-up.
3. Have the feedback conversation.
4. Review: what worked well, what didn't?
5. What do you need to focus on to improve your next feedback conversation?

Accept all responses to feedback

Despite good planning and execution, you may find that your feedback is not met with hugs and roses – or even with a simple thank you. It is easier to give feedback when there is a receptive listener. It is more challenging if your feedback meets with resistance of some kind. But by accepting all responses to feedback, even outright rejection, it is possible to foster acceptance and to embed a culture of feedback.

Don't push back against any resistance. Open up the opportunity to have a conversation to deepen your understanding. Move *with* the push, take it into a dance. What's the source of the resistance? How does the resistance help you to give better feedback? What else do you need to do or to know?

If you're developing a new emphasis on feedback, then expect resistance and scepticism. What would be in your team member's mind? 'Is this a once-off?' 'Is this something I can avoid?' 'It won't last...'

Keep in your mind: 'How will I stay calm?' 'How can I better understand the resistance?' 'What's another way to say this?'

Our usual response to resistance is to push back. We can be caught off-guard. We lose our balance, feel surprised, dominated, defensive, resentful, angry or hurt. We match the resistance.

Resistance isn't usually an end point. It's a weigh station on the path to acceptance. As the coach, you have the opportunity to take a generous mindset. As you develop your understanding of how the path of resistance works, pay more attention to the responses you receive. Even though the initial response to tough feedback might be resistance, with patience you may move through to acceptance. Make sure you are in charge of the direction you are going in. Identify where you are at on the resistance and acceptance path (see Figure 9.3). Keep the conversation focused on moving forward. How can you provide support to help movement along the path?

Figure 9.3 – The feedback acceptance path

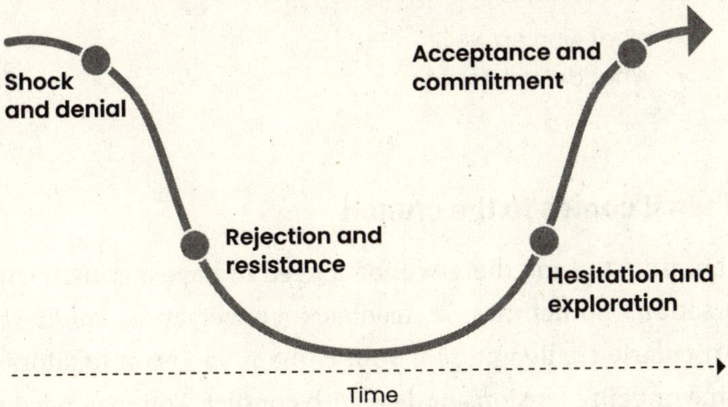

Resistance can be caused by insecurity, lack of knowledge and fear of change. You can help people to move through their own personal cycle of change in response to feedback, and the organisation's broader change programs. Notice how people respond to change, and adapt your responses so that they can move forward.

Activity

1. What is your usual response to resistance?
2. Map out an upcoming conversation so that you are ready to work with resistance. Or review a past conversation to identify what you would do differently if you were to have the conversation again.
   - How would you listen differently?
   - How could you be more accepting of resistance?
   - When might you have asked for their view?
   - How might you have been more accepting of their view (even without agreeing)?
   - How might you ask for suggestions on what to do next?

3. If you work on an upcoming conversation, come back here to review:
   - What worked well?
   - What did you learn?

When it comes to the crunch

From time to time there will be a need to have a crunch conversation. Sometimes, a feedback conversation might be particularly challenging for you. Perhaps you want to address some ongoing tensions or deal with conflict. You may need to give a tough performance review or say no to someone in need. You may need to confront disrespectful behaviour, disagree with a majority view or ask for a pay rise. For some of us, these conversations can be quite challenging to face up to.

A crunch conversation is one that requires some courage: it's anything you find hard to talk about. Crunch conversations change the tension or 'stuckness' between people. Their purpose is to take the relationship to a new and better place.

Left to themselves, small embers of discord and dissatisfaction can smoulder and flare up. You can become consumed by putting out little fires. If you act to put out the little fires you may evoke fear, but you are extinguishing the flames and preventing a major burn.

Self-manage your own response to conflict so that you avoid less and over-react less. Better manage your own fight–flight response. And always in coaching mode help others to better manage their responses.

As Nelson Mandela's wisdom reminds us: "'*Courage is not the absence of fear, misgiving or self-doubt, but action in their presence.*"

What is a challenging conversation?

A challenging conversation might be necessary if you:

- Feel your self-esteem is affected.
- Experience the issue at stake as important yet you are uncertain of the outcome.
- Feel concerned that someone you care about has been wounded, let down or upset in some way.
- Find yourself bad-mouthing or gossiping about someone else, or know someone is doing that about you.
- Feel strong negative emotion when thinking about the other person, for example anger, sadness, regret, indignation.
- Feel helpless or stranded in the relationship.
- Shut down communication with another.
- Feel deeply about an issue.

Margaret Heffernan reinforces a couple of critical points in her TED Talk, 'Dare to Disagree', which is well worth watching[42]. The first is the value of taking a long-term perspective – see the crunch conversation in the context of the ongoing relationship. The second is that at least some conversations are crunchy because they require us to work with opposed perspectives. They are worth sticking with to achieve high-value innovation and learning.

Activity

1. How do you rate your courage at proceeding in the face of challenge?

Very low	Quite low	Average	Quite high	Very high

2. What do you usually do when you experience challenging situations?
3. How good are you at having difficult conversations?

Very bad	Quite bad	Average	Quite good	Very good

4. What do you think you need to be better at to improve the way you have difficult conversations?
5. What are the risks of *not* acting?

Identify when a crunch conversation is needed

If you know what triggers you, you can move quickly to have a crunch conversation that will recover the relationship. By knowing your triggers, you can also manage them better and avoid feeling conflict. If you are aware of what your triggers are, you can become better at keeping your own safety catch on.

What triggers conflict and why we avoid it

What are your triggers for conflict? What is it that makes a conversation challenging for you? When you are in the heat of the conversation, how do these triggers affect your ability to achieve the outcomes you need? What happens to your coaching when you are triggered?

We may avoid crunch conversations when we feel some sense of threat. David Rock suggests that understanding the human approach–avoid system is a powerful way to make sense of how we respond to threat[43].

When we encounter something we perceive to be good, we approach it and over time learn that it has rewarding effects. When we experience something as good or enjoyable, we produce the hormone dopamine, which is associated with feelings of pleasure, interest, solutions, extension, wholeness and engagement.

The same pattern occurs with things we perceive to be negative. Engaging with conflict usually becomes associated with negative emotions and punishment. Threat/avoidance produces the hormone cortisol. Cortisol is associated with feelings of pain, uncertainty, problems, contraction, tunnel vision and disengagement. We attempt to avoid these kinds of feelings and so we are inclined to avoid challenging conversations.

When people sense a threat, their cognitive resources diminish. They don't notice subtle signals, errors increase and their response is more likely to be defensive. Small stressors may magnify. When we work with others, the avoidance response is much stronger, it occurs more rapidly and lasts longer than the approach response.

To help minimise this, identify what is most likely to trigger an avoidance response in you. David Rock calls these the SCARF areas; which of these social connections generates the strongest threat response in you?

- **Status** – perception of your relative social standing or seniority

- **Certainty** – confidence that prediction is possible and you know what is happening moment to moment
- **Autonomy** – ability to exert control over the environment and to make your own choices
- **Relatedness** – your sense of belonging to particular social groups and whether we/they are friend or foe
- **Fairness** – a sense of justice and transparency.

You can assess yourself against the SCARF threats here: https://neuroleadership.com/scarf-assessment/.

Which threat is most salient for you? How might this influence how you approach conflict? What influence does it have on individual team members? How does it relate to the issues you find most challenging to coach?

Also consider what seem to be the triggers for the person you are experiencing conflict with, or the person you are coaching. Is the conflict about your relative seniority and importance? Do you experience conflict because you perceive there is a sense of injustice or a lack of fairness? Is the other person 'being difficult' because they are unable to exert a sense of control over their environment and choices are being made for them?

Activity

1. Assess your conflict triggers. Complete the online self-assessment of the SCARF areas that matter most to you.
2. What triggers you?
3. What do you do when triggered?
4. What do you avoid doing, to avoid being triggered?

5. What do you overdo?
6. What action could you take to reduce the power of your triggers?

Work on the pinch to avoid the crunch

By being alert to conflict triggers, it is possible to reduce the frequency and magnitude of conflict.

Being more aware of triggers means that we can better tune in to potential crunch points.

Being more attuned to triggers which lead to pinch points is useful if you want to better manage relationships and minimise conflict[44]. A pinch is an opportunity to have a conversation about expectations, resolve differences and avoid a crunch. Noticing and responding at a pinch point is a better time to manage others' expectations and to recalibrate responses. If we let conflict continue, we may experience more serious conflict later.

The model in Figure 9.4 overleaf is based on the model developed by John J. Sherwood and John C. Glidewell[44]. It outlines the dynamics of conversations over time. It highlights the importance of having difficult conversations at the pinch point, rather than waiting to get to a crunch point. While we might feel the pinch, the common tendency is to ignore or avoid it. Doing so increases the likelihood that we will come to a crunch point, where the stakes are much higher and the conversation is more difficult. The goal is to find the courage to have conversations at pinch points to uncover issues, disagreements and concerns. Doing so realigns expectations.

Figure 9.4 – Conversation dynamics

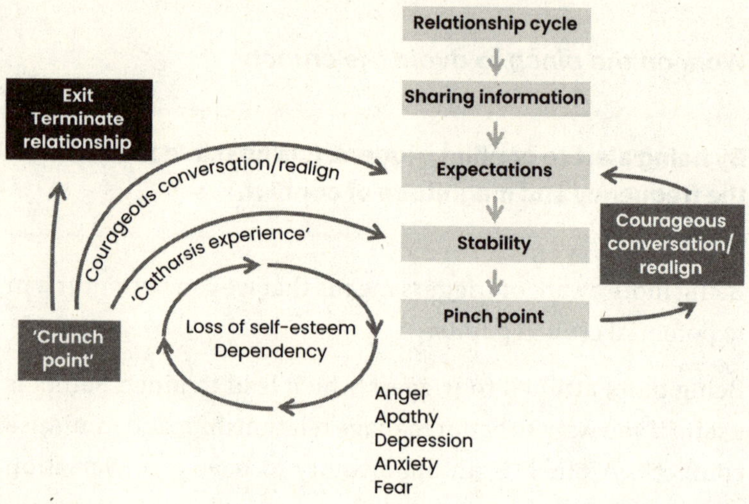

Relationships go through familiar cycles. We begin by sharing information. And then we either set or develop expectations about the relationship and how it works. Generally, relationships then go through a period of stability and the relationship creates value for us.

At some point, we may experience a pinch. This is a disruption, which may arise because one party doesn't behave as the other expects. Or the disruption may be caused externally, for example by a new person joining the team or a reallocation of resources. At this point, there are two options.

The first is that there is a period of uncertainty about the relationship. If this continues, it may lead to a shift in the relationship, so that its continuance reduces self-esteem or causes dependency. Feelings about the relationship become negative. If this continues with enough intensity, and is not addressed, it may come to a crunch point. Then the relationship may be abandoned. It may be easier to let it go than attempt to recover it.

Or there may be a 'catharsis experience', one that allows the letting off of steam and then the relationship returns to a state of stability. This may relieve the anxiety, but often doesn't solve the problem in the relationship.

A third alternative is that a courageous conversation is held that recognises the problems in the relationship. The purpose of the conversation is to realign it by clarifying and renegotiating expectations.

The second option for action at a pinch point is to engage in a courageous conversation to realign expectations at the moment the pinch is felt. Opting for courageous conversations at pinch points helps to avoid crunch points. It avoids too many negotiations when 'under fire', when so much more is at stake.

Are you feeling any pinch or crunch points in your relationships right now? What topics do you find hard to talk about? With whom? How does this impact your relationship with the specific person? Are there broader impacts outside this relationship?

Which of your conversations/relationships take you into the zone where you feel the heat, but stay open and compassionate? Which of your conversations/relationships take you into a red zone, where you hold your ground but feel you may risk the relationship, or where you find it difficult to hold your ground?

Activity

1. Identify any pinch points in your relationships. What action could you take now to avoid them turning into crunch points?
2. Do you notice any pinch points in your team? What action could you take now to avoid them turning into crunch points?
3. How do you usually respond when you reach a crunch point?
4. Are you experiencing any crunch points now? What will you do?

How to have a crunch conversation

If you follow a specific crunch conversation structure, it will reduce your anxiety and achieve better outcomes.

Remind yourself of your coaching mindset. That will help you to switch your thinking from from judging to inviting. Reduce the judge in you, reduce your certainty and instead adopt a learning, curious stance as you prepare for your crunch conversation.

By being more mindful about how you approach crunch conversations, you can increase your effectiveness. The shift from resistance to receptivity is relevant here too. Orient yourself towards moving forward; turn your resistance into a dance.

The final activity in this chapter is an eight-step formula for having a crunch point conversation. It will help you to prepare for an upcoming conversation. Think through the structure for your conversation. You may find it useful to rehearse with a trusted colleague/friend before the conversation takes place.

Activity

1. **Name the issue:** What's the issue you want to resolve? Describe it clearly and specifically.
2. **Bring an example:** What is/are examples of how this issue shows up?
3. **Impact:** What's the impact of this issue on you/others?
4. **Your contribution:** How have you personally contributed to this issue?
5. **Step into their shoes:** How would you feel if you were in their shoes?
6. **Your intention:** What's your intention in raising, addressing and trying to resolve the issue?
7. **Enrol them:** How could you enrol them in that outcome?
8. **Complete the conversation:** What else needs to be raised or said to complete the conversation?

After your crunch conversation, review the outcome.

1. What worked well?
2. What didn't go quite to plan? Did that help or hinder things?
3. What, if anything, knocked you off balance during the conversation?
4. What insight did you gain about yourself in preparing and having the crunch conversation?
5. How could you improve your experience for the future?

10

Cheer like a coach

As a coach you have the opportunity to make a big difference to the motivation of your team members. Cheer their progress and notice the difference it makes.

The single most important factor in engaging people in their jobs is the perception that they believe they are making progress in meaningful work. When people experience a sense of progress, they are more intrinsically motivated. Their interest in and enjoyment of the work itself becomes the strongest motivator. Even quite small progress steps can make a big difference.

+ Giving individual praise is the best motivator

One of Martin's early learnings coaching his son's under-12 soccer team was that he couldn't criticise them. It deflated them. What worked best was to give the young players a lot of praise. This meant he needed to pay attention to each individual. He needed to know what small piece of progress they had made in that day's game, so that he could name it for them. He needed to know what motivated each person and let that guide his praise for them.

He set his own target that he would strive to help each team member become 5% to 10% better. He thought that if each player could keep improving in small increments, continually getting better, the team would be better.

Martin didn't want to focus on the best players; it was about the whole team, and every player. He's trying to instil that same discipline in the team members. He uses a Kris Kringle-style process. Each team member pulls a secret name out of the hat before the game and then has to praise that player during the game. After the game, the team tries to guess who picked whose name from the hat based on the praise they saw each one give. It's a bit of fun, with a serious intent: to make praise a constant and make everyone responsible for it.

Martin says it's so much easier to criticise when things go wrong. He has noticed in the soccer team, as well as back in his office, that it is easy to point out what's going wrong. It is so much harder to point out when someone has done a good thing.

What he wants to create is an experience that is always enjoyable and fun. It's not so much about the winning, but whether team members enjoy each others' company and get a positive experience from playing the game together.

What can you do to make sure your team members come to work each day ready to do and be their best? How do you best motivate your team? Is there a magic formula that can release higher levels of motivation? What is motivation? And as a coach how can you nurture it?

Work motivation has been the subject of long-standing debate. Teresa Amabile and Steve Kramer have researched how motivation works and this chapter draws on their work[18]. There's a strong evidence base to their approach. They suggest some very practical steps you can take to increase your own and your team's motivation. In the case study above, what Martin was doing intuitively with his soccer team was using some of the best principles of motivation.

Here is a list of five motivators that came out of a survey of 669 managers from companies around the world:

1. Recognition for good work
2. Tangible incentives such as pay
3. Support for making progress in the work
4. Interpersonal support
5. Having clear goals.

Which of these five do you believe has the biggest effect on motivation?

Recognition for good work ranked number one. While recognition does boost motivation, the work by Amabile and Kramer shows that making progress does it to a far greater extent. Support for making progress was answered as number one by only 5% of managers in the survey cited above. What we *believe* motivates people isn't what *actually* motivates them day to day. Cheering matters. But it's how you cheer that matters most.

Cheer to trigger progress experiences

What does it mean to cheer your team?

Amabile and Kramer's research explored the motivations and performance of 238 project workers. They worked in seven companies across three different industries. Daily diaries were kept and analysed. They ended up with 12,000 individual diary reports that allowed an in-depth look at how people experience their working day.

The key findings were:

- Negative events were five times more powerful than positive events in their impact on mood. As we've already established, people expend more cognitive and emotional energy on bad events than good events.
- People regularly underestimate their emotional reactions to events. Even apparently mundane events exert a potent influence: 28% of small events triggered large and lasting emotional reactions.
- People recall more negative actions by their leaders than positive ones, more intensely, and in more detail. The impact of your actions is bigger than you think.

When asked to identify what triggered a 'best day' experience, 76% identified progress in the work by the person or their team. On progress days, people were more intrinsically motivated by interest in and enjoyment of the work itself. The amount of progress was often quite minor.

When asked to identify a 'worst day' experience, 67% identified a setback in the work by the person or their team.

People's immediate emotional responses to events are often much bigger than they realise. The diaries showed that events that people thought were unimportant were often highly motivating. Or if they were perceived negatively, they were highly demotivating. Small positive and negative events serve as tiny 'booster shots' that improve or decrease motivation.

The good news for leaders is that it is not necessary to do 'big things' to influence the mood and motivation of others. Sweating the small stuff matters. Small actions have far greater power than we know[45].

Amabile likens this to playing video games[18]. Noticing small amounts of progress is like the bars in video games. Anyone who plays video games knows the bars that denote progress through the levels in the game are extremely motivating. They are always on screen so that you know exactly where you are in the levels, what it will take to get to the next level, and the overall goal. The best leaders use small pieces of recognition in the same way. They let people know what progress they have made, where they are up to and remind them of the overall goal.

Activity

1. How do you pay attention to the motivation and commitment of your team?
2. What is your biggest problem when you spend face-to-face time motivating your people?
3. How well do you know your team members' perceptions of what it's like to work at your organisation?
4. How well do you know how your team is feeling (their mood, state)?
5. What do you know of what intrinsically motivates each member of your team?

Progress experiences improve 'inner work life'

How we think and feel about events affects our level of motivation for work. The more people experience a sense of progress, the more likely they are to stay motivated, and to be creatively productive. Motivation affects what work we do, how much effort we put into it and how long we persist at it.

We react to everything that happens to us at work. We make judgments about how important our work is, how much effort it takes and how much effort we will put in to it. We decide whether we like the people we work with and whether our bosses are competent. We spend a great deal of our time at work. Much of how we see our success as individuals is tied to our day-to-day experience of work. If people don't feel their work is valued, if they don't feel pride or happiness in their work, then they will have little drive to perform.

If you pay attention to what sense people make of their experiences and how they feel at work, you can increase their motivation. You can have more influence over both the well-being and the work output of your team. This is what Amabile and Kramer call 'Inner Work Life' (see Figure 10.1 which was adapted from their Figure 2-1)[18].

Figure 10.1 – Adaptation of Amabile and Kramer's 'inner work life'

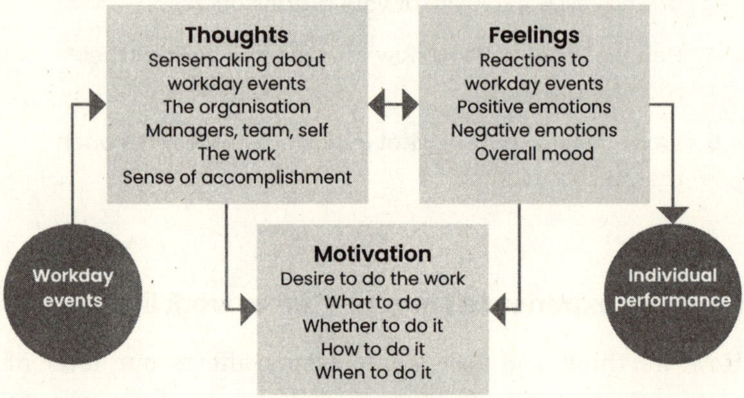

Most people's inner work life changes on the basis of the events they experience (rather than their personality).

How any event is perceived depends on individual experiences. Different people respond differently to the same experience depending on how they make sense of it. What one person thinks about an event now is informed partly by what has happened to them in the past and what it meant to them then. For example, if your boss tells you that you will shortly have additional resources to assist with a time-pressured project, you will view this as helpful. If the boss has said this in the past, but the resources didn't eventuate, you may see it as another way in which your boss lets you down.

Even if we start the day in a bad mood that can change. Making positive sense of something that someone else does, or successfully accomplishing a task, can improve our mood. Emotions are generally felt in the moment and shift quite fluidly. The way we've made sense of the boss's actions affects our mood. We feel reassured and re-energised when we believe there will be more support. Or we feel demoralised and cheated when we hear a promise we don't believe will be kept.

The sense we make of events affects feelings.

We know about the power of the positive, and it's reinforced here. Feeling positive at work:

- Increases flexibility in problem solving and negotiation by 50%
- Flows on to the next day; the more positive a person's mood on one day, the more creativity there is the next day
- Leads to more favourable performance evaluations and larger pay increases.

Our thoughts and feelings about an event affect our motivation. Motivation is a combination of three things; the choice to do something, desire to expend effort on it and drive to continue putting in the effort.

There are three kinds of motivation:

1. **Extrinsic motivation.** This is the drive to do something to get something else, such as more pay, a bonus, a promotion or access to desired resources. Take care with extrinsic motivators. They are strong and salient, and this is the challenge. They can *undermine* intrinsic motivation. Just spending five minutes focusing on extrinsic motivation temporarily lowers creativity.
2. **Intrinsic motivation.** Intrinsic motivation is the drive to do something because it is interesting, enjoyable, or challenging.
3. **Relational motivation.** This is the drive to do something because it builds relationships with people we like and respect.

Intrinsic motivation is the lever that presents the greatest opportunity to leaders. And when done well it grows relational motivation. You become the boss that people love to work with!

Inner work life is a system of thoughts, feelings and motivations. We respond to events in particular ways. How we make sense of and feel about them affects our motivation. Motivation has the strongest impact on performance. Studies show that people perform better when they are satisfied, happier, and intrinsically motivated.

How you can improve inner work life for your team

How can you use your deeper knowledge of motivation to improve performance?

There are three important ways to affect inner work life: a sense of progress, catalysts and nourishers. A coaching style allows you to develop a deeper understanding of what will help motivate each particular individual in your team. You can promote progress, provide catalysts and nourish your team members (see Figure 10.2).

Figure 10.2 – Ways to improve inner work life

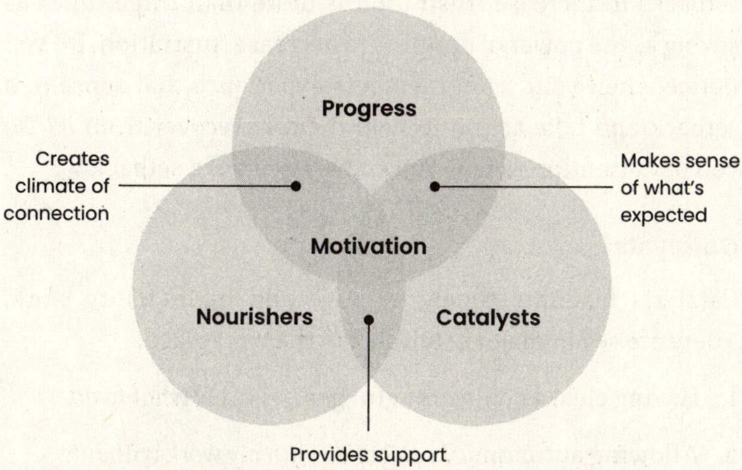

The Progress Principle

Progress triggers positive emotions like satisfaction, happiness, joy and gladness. Making headway on meaningful work improves inner work life and boosts long-term performance. It creates a positive loop: positive inner work life creates progress, which creates positive inner work life.

So, as a part of any work, it's important that you provide feedback, that you notice the efforts and results of your team's work. How do they know they're making progress? What feedback do you give them on their progress? How often do you do this? How good are you at noticing and celebrating their progress?

How can you increase the 'video-gaming' element in your team's work day?

As noted above, bad is stronger than good; the power of the negative far outweighs that of the positive. The power of setbacks to increase frustration is more than three times as strong as the power of progress to decrease frustration. Do you notice when your team members experience that sense of a setback and take action to help them to recover from it? Do you pay attention to how you convey news of a setback?

Catalysts

Catalysts facilitate timely, creative and high-quality work. There are seven major catalysts[18] in the workplace:

1. Having clear and meaningful goals. *I know what to do.*
2. Allowing autonomy. *I can get on with my work without undue oversight.*
3. Providing sufficient resources. *I have the resources I need to do my work.*
4. Giving enough (but not too much) time, to get work done. *I can get the work done in the time expected.*
5. Help with the work from managers and colleagues. *I know I will get help when I ask for it.*
6. Learning from problems and successes. *I keep learning and improving.*
7. Allowing ideas to flow. *I can contribute my ideas.*

There are three main ways for you to shape the availability of catalysts for your team. First, you can show good consideration for people and their ideas. You can also make sure systems and procedures are well coordinated and, thirdly, you can ensure clear, honest, respectful and free-flowing communication occurs.

Some of the failures of leadership that you should avoid include:

- Creating ambiguity
- Unclear, overlapping or duplicated accountabilities
- Telling different people different reasons for tasks
- Encouraging people two layers down to speak directly to you about problems
- Not being aware of and/or not managing team tensions
- Underestimating the likelihood and significance of interpersonal problems
- Not noticing erosion of trust.

The overall organisational climate also shapes the availability of catalysts. Yet by far the strongest influence is the direct relationship of team members with their line manager.

Unclear goals, too much control and insufficient resources inhibit progress and motivation. If leaders remove these barriers, people's own intrinsic motivation will get the job done.

Nourishers

You nourish the inner work life of your team members when you recognise, encourage and support them. Help them to resolve interpersonal conflict. Provide opportunities for people to know each other better and to celebrate and have fun. These all nourish the human connection.

Nourishment comes from:

- Showing respect
- Giving encouragement
- Providing emotional support
- Growing affiliation.

A lack of attention to nourishers can mean that there are spill-over effects, with conflict and contagion from bad moods spreading. This contributes to a toxic climate in the workplace. Move quickly to contain the spread.

If you are coaching your team members, you will be nourishing them too.

The power of a daily checklist

The better your own inner work life, the better able you are to pay attention to the inner work life of your team and other stakeholders. There is a positive flow-on impact on the inner work life of the team.

A very useful strategy for managing your own progress is to review your day for five minutes at the end of each day. In fact, when line managers' diaries were examined their greatest sense of progress came when their team members reported that they had made progress. Why not start with yourself?

Atul Gawande showed that even experienced surgeons can improve their performance dramatically. Using a simple checklist to guide every single operation reduces error[18]. The items on the checklist are quite mundane; they are just what needs to be done. In a three-month experiment in eight different hospitals the rate of complications fell by 36% when surgeons used checklists.

Any complex task, not just surgery, requires a regular check of all the fundamentals. That liberates the team to focus on the work and be ready for anything unexpected that might arise.

Motivation matters. A sense of progress motivates people to accept difficult challenges more readily. They will persist longer at tougher challenges if they feel motivated, and feel more satisfied when they meet the challenges. When people feel positive and capable, they see problems as positive. They believe they will succeed.

The key lesson to take away from understanding motivation is that as long as work is meaningful, we don't have to do a lot to motivate others to excel at it.

Activity

1. Consider one salient event that happened to you yesterday at work, the first thing that comes to mind.
2. Your thinking: How did you interpret it? What sense did you make of it?
3. Your feeling: How did it make you feel? What emotions were evoked and what was your mood overall?
4. Your motivation: How did it affect your motivation? Was it an event that evoked a positive emotion or a negative one? Was it about you, or was someone else involved?

5. How did it impact on your performance?
6. Create your daily diary to keep you focused on creating progress for your team.

What coaches can do to improve motivation

Facilitating a sense of progress may be the most powerful thing that leaders can do. Coaching provides a great base for this.

Focusing inner work life to create a sense of progress builds motivation

Mary had international experience with a top-10 global organisation in her industry and had been attracted to her current Australian organisation with the promise of a very senior role. Once she arrived in the organisation, the promised role had disappeared. She was placed into a specially created role with responsibility for a series of significant, high-profile projects and a couple of small teams to manage.

Eighteen months on and she was experiencing conflict. She had made a big commitment to join the organisation yet her expectations were not met. She had a sense of having to 'do time' while waiting for the big opportunity. She had completed several projects and was being told to bide her time. Her engagement in working with her peers and her sense of accomplishment in her achievements were reducing. She felt frustrated, angry, depressed and her motivation both for work and to the organisation were diminishing.

Mary had recently discovered that she was not in the organisation's designated high-potential program.

This disappointed her greatly and led to a downward spiral in motivation and performance.

Mary was making sense of the context as one in which she was not making any progress, and she had come to view herself as quite stuck. She viewed the organisation and her line manager as unsupportive. She no longer believed that the organisation would deliver on its promise, which had become vaguer over time.

Her emotions were low. She felt betrayed by the senior organisational leader who had recruited her and who had identified himself as her mentor. Her trust was reducing. Her self confidence was also eroding. Despite a genuine desire to realise her ambitions, she felt unable to let go of frustration and disappointment.

Initial coaching conversations focused on identifying new ways to make sense of what was happening. What was happening in the organisation? What was happening for Mary personally in terms of her feelings and motivations? We focused on making more constructive sense of the situation. Mary mapped out several courses of action, including leaving the organisation. This helped her to feel less stuck and powerless.

When she wasn't weighed down by negativity, she used her own intrinsic motivation to fuel her work and sense of success. She was able to celebrate the fact that one of her successful projects was the turn-around of a project that had long been regarded as a 'poisoned chalice'.

In our coaching context, we were only able to shift the way she thought and felt about her situation. By freeing up her ability to make sense of some things and helping her to be more positive, she was able to increase her own motivation. Using her daily diary, she was able to notice the progress she was making.

Actions that take away meaning and purpose, or having work or ideas dismissed, can have a big impact. Even super smart people and top performers like Mary can't make progress each day without the support of their leaders.

Employee satisfaction and perceptions of their organisations, their leaders and their colleagues matter.

When people are happy and motivated they are more productive and they have a more positive outlook.

Focusing inner work life to create a sense of progress builds motivation, empowerment and productivity.

Activity

Pay attention to your team members' motivation levels.

1. What happened today that was positive for the team?
    - Which one or two events today indicated either a small win or a possible breakthrough?
    - Did team members have enough autonomy to solve problems and take ownership of the project?
    - Did you show respect to team members? Did you recognise their contributions to progress, attend to their ideas and treat them as trusted professionals?
2. What happened today that was negative for the team?
    - Which one or two events today indicated either a small setback or a possible crisis?
    - Were team members overly constrained in their ability to solve problems and feel ownership of the project?

- Did you disrespect any team members? Did you fail to recognise their contributions to progress, not attend to their ideas, or not treat them as trusted professionals?

3. What indications of the quality of your team members' inner work lives did you notice today?

Afterword

Leaders model coaching in an 'everyone coaches' culture

Before I leave you, I wanted to share some further examples of how leading like a coach works in practice and to include some final advice to ensure that when you move towards a coaching model in your team or your organisation, you have the best chance of making it a success.

A coaching culture balances the need to deliver results now with the need to deliver results in the future.

A coaching style reinforces a flexible culture that is guided by purpose and learning, where people welcome change rather than stability[46]. They care about the future and are open and agile. Coaching embodies these features. This creates an affinity between the means and the end: you coach a coaching culture into reality.

You have a coaching culture if:

- Senior leaders believe in coaching, and coach;
- Leaders look for opportunities to help others learn;
- Leaders ask open questions rather than tell the solution;
- People willingly give and receive feedback; and
- People have honest and open conversations.

If coaching isn't a priority for managers, then you know you don't have a coaching culture in your organisation.

Creating a coaching culture

The best coaching cultures are those where leaders use a coaching style with their teams. When leaders are coaching, and their teams are learning that this is how we do things here, a coaching style becomes pervasive. Anyone can coach, anytime.

Team members can take the opportunity to have coaching conversations with their bosses, peers can use the coaching style as they engage with each other, and so on. Coaching behaviours in these contexts take a conversational form. The responsibility is to maintain and articulate a developmental, action-oriented frame of reference.

A coaching culture supports leaders who coach. As coach, you focus on 'filling everyone else's bucket', as Alex says. It is as important to keep yourself replenished. In a coaching culture, support, encouragement and replenishment comes from those around you. Create a circle of like-minded coaching advocates. Make a commitment to meet on a regular basis to coach each other on your own development and wellbeing.

A culture characterised by coaching has within it the seeds to create a sustainable, self-generating leadership legacy. By being deliberately developmental[12], a coaching culture grows future leaders as it empowers and develops current leaders. It's not just leaders who coach. Anyone in any role at any level can also take a coaching approach. This creates an 'everyone coaches' culture[47].

Moving towards a culture of care

A large, global mining company is shifting to a coaching culture. The poor results of its last culture survey galvanised the company into action. It wants to develop a learning culture that is based on coaching and feedback. But you can't just say it. You need to embed it in every program and policy, in every conversation that leaders have. And senior leaders need to role model the coaching culture.

As a technical, engineering-focused company, they 'want to get things done and to know the answers'. They have prided themselves on being a FLMGSD (flexible, low maintenance, get sh@* done) kind of place. So it makes sense that there was not a lot of coaching happening.

The focus of their shift was to a culture of care. What a radical shift! Care has become the foundation for their values. It's unusual for a mining company to want to develop a culture of care: yet they don't see it as being 'touchy feely'. For senior leaders, it's about accountability. The company's leadership believe that if they don't care for staff, shareholders and the community, they won't deliver their results. Care is the wellspring for delivering results. They have developed a strong business case around care.

On a day-to-day level, for them, care means learning and development. This translates into regular coaching conversations between managers and their teams. They believe that frequent on-the-job coaching can do more to build a learning culture than anything else. They are developing their managers to have conversations that build trust. For their leaders, this means genuinely asking people how they are going. Being less focused on the task and what they have done. This is not off the agenda, but it isn't the whole agenda. What have you learnt? What could I have done to help you? What can I do to help you?

They are encouraging their leaders to be vulnerable. Again, in a mining company, this is not easy. They have made it practical. To be vulnerable as a leader means to ask for feedback and reflect on what you heard. Leaders are seeing that their job is not just to direct but to coach and mentor more. They report that the conversations they are having are more open and less threatening for people.

Sarah, the Organisational Development leader managing the change program in the case study above, says that once people have the 'aha' moment of coaching rather than controlling, it is much easier. An engineer heading up a local committee was frustrated because people weren't volunteering and engaging in the work of the committee. Things weren't going to plan. With some coaching, he understood how to identify and engage his key influencers to form his agenda. He had a massive win at his next committee meeting, where plans were agreed and progress was achieved. The difference between controlling and coaching now made sense – he got it. The value became clear. He was able to connect with people, gain support and achieve his goals. Giving up control made it easier to get what he needed.

Leaders need to role model a coaching culture

The company is aware that what leaders role model is what drives culture. They are injecting leaders who model coaching into work sites to help with the cultural integration. Controlling and domineering leaders don't last. The company's message is that 'if you want to be part of this organisation, we have a code and expectations about how everyone behaves'.

They have let some people go who were not the right kind of leader. People around them can see this, it makes the culture and the code tangible. It encourages those who are 'border-line' to shape up. It encourages those who do the right thing to develop their confidence. It encourages those who are good at it to become role models for their colleagues.

While it's early days, and a follow-up survey is underway as we go to print, Sarah reports that there is a different kind of energy. There have been much more proactive conversations from the leaders, starting at the very top level. *'There is an exciting vibe and energy from the senior leaders. While it's a culture change, it has paradoxically simplified things for them. It's clear why we're doing this, what needs to be done to succeed, and it is rewarding to do it'.*

Alex's organisation (see the case study in Chapter 3) recently won a national award as a 'best employer' and are renowned for their 'great company culture'. They work hard to create an organisation where people want to do their best work and are fulfilled in doing it. They have had a strong and consistent focus on encouraging a coaching style as underpinning the way for leaders to engage with their people. They can measure the impact of this not just in engagement but also in performance. It is now creating its own momentum, becoming self-generating.

Coaching, not controlling, is a compelling way for leaders to improve the team's performance. Leaders who coach create and grow trust. When trust is high, people are engaged and energised. They work harder, longer, and produce more.

Activity

1. Assess the extent to which your organisation has a coaching culture. Do senior leaders:
    - Believe in coaching
    - Coach
    - Look for opportunities to help others learn
    - Ask open questions rather than tell the solution
    - Appear willing to give and receive feedback
    - Have honest and open conversations?
2. Your organisation's coaching culture strengths:
3. Your organisation's coaching culture gaps:
4. What is the culture that you are reinforcing in your own team? Do you:
    - Believe in coaching
    - Coach
    - Look for opportunities to help others learn
    - Ask open questions rather than tell the solution
    - Appear willing to give and receive feedback
    - Have honest and open conversations?
5. Your coaching culture strengths:
6. Your coaching culture gaps:
7. What action might you be able to take to contribute to supporting a coaching culture?

References

1. Taylor, F.W. *The Principles of Scientific Management*. 1911, New York and London: Harper & Brothers.
2. Clifton, J. *Declining Global Productivity Growth: The Fix*. The Chairman's Blog, Gallup News, 2017 [18 October 2017]. Available from: http://news.gallup.com/opinion/chairman/220472/declining-global-productivity-growth-fix.aspx.
3. Turner, C. and McCarthy, G. *Coachable moments: Identifying factors that influence managers to take advantage of coachable moments in day-to-day management*. International Journal of Evidence Based Coaching and Mentoring, 2015. 13(1): p. 1-13.
4. Nink, M. and Robison, J. *The Damage Inflicted by Poor Managers*. Business Journal, Gallup News, 2016 [20 December 2016]. Available from: http://news.gallup.com/businessjournal/200108/damage-inflicted-poor-managers.aspx.
5. Aon Hewitt. *2017 Trends in Global Employee Engagement*. 2017. Available from: https://www.aonhewitt.com.au/Home/Resources/Reports-and-research/2017-Trends-in-Global-Employee-Engagement-report.
6. Harter, J.K., et al. *The Relationship between Engagement at Work and Organizational Outcomes: 2016 Q12 Meta-analysis: Ninth Edition*. 2016: Gallup, Inc. Available from: https://news.gallup.com/reports/191489/q12-meta-analysis-report-2016.aspx.
7. Emond, L. 2 *Reasons Why Employee Engagement Programs Fall Short*. Opinion, Gallup News, 2017 [15 August 2017]. Available from: http://news.gallup.com/opinion/gallup/216155/reasons-why-employee-engagement-programs-fall-short.aspx.
8. Gallup, Inc. *State of the Global Workplace: Executive Summary*. 2017: Washington, D.C. Available from: http://news.gallup.com/reports/220313/state-global-workplace-2017.aspx.

9. Clifton, J. *The World's Broken Workplace*. The Chairman's Blog, Gallup News, 2017 [13 June 2017]; Available from: http://news.gallup.com/opinion/chairman/212045/world-broken-workplace.aspx.

10. Clifton, J. *Are You Sure You Have a Great Workplace Culture?* The Chairman's Blog, Gallup News, 2017 [27 April 2017]. Available from: http://news.gallup.com/opinion/chairman/209033/sure-great-workplace-culture.aspx.

11. Beck, R. and Harter, J. *Why Good Managers Are So Rare*. Harvard Business Review, 13 March 2014. Available from: https://hbr.org/2014/03/why-good-managers-are-so-rare.

12. Kegan, R. and Lahey, L. *An Everyone Culture: Becoming a Deliberately Developmental Organization*. 2016, Boston: Harvard Business Review Press.

13. Rock, D. and Donde, R. *Driving organizational change with internal coaching programs: part one*. Industrial and Commercial Training, 2008. 40(1): p. 10-18.

14. Zak, P.J. *The neuroscience of trust*. Harvard Business Review, January-February 2017. Available from: https://hbr.org/2017/01/the-neuroscience-of-trust.

15. Garvey Berger, J. and Johnston, K. *Simple Habits for Complex Times: Powerful Practices for Leaders*. 2015, Redwood City: Stanford University Press.

16. Anthony, E.L., *The impact of leadership coaching on leadership behaviors*. Journal of Management Development, 2017. 36(7): p. 930-939.

17. Kolb, D.A. and Kolb, A.Y. *The Kolb Learning Style Inventory 4.0: Guide to Theory, Psychometrics, Research & Applications*. 2013: Experience Based Learning Systems. Available from: https://learningfromexperience.com/downloads/research-library/the-kolb-learning-style-inventory-4-0.pdf

18. Amabile, T. and Kramer, S. *The Progress Principle: Using Small Wins to Ignite Joy, Engagement, and Creativity at Work*. 2011, Boston: Harvard Business Review Press.

19. Flaherty, J. *Coaching: Evoking Excellence in Others*. Third ed. 2010, London and New York: Routledge.

20. Brown, B. *The power of vulnerability*. TEDxHouston, 2011. Available from: https://youtu.be/iCvmsMzlF7o.

21. Thomas, E. *Empathy sayings and quotes*. Available from: http://www.wiseoldsayings.com/empathy-quotes/.

22. Goleman, D. *The Focused Leader*. Harvard Business Review, 2013. December: p. 51-59.

23. David, S. *The gift and power of emotional courage*. TEDWomen 2017. Available from: https://www.ted.com/talks/susan_david_the_gift_and_power_of_emotional_courage.

24. Schein, E.H. *Humble Inquiry: The Gentle Art of Asking Instead of Telling*. 2013, Oakland, Ca.: Berrett-Koehler Publishers.

25. Senge, P.M., Kleiner, A. and Roberts, C. *The Fifth Discipline Fieldbook: Strategies and tools for building a learning organization*. 1994, London: Nicholas Brealey.

26. Kegan, R. and Lahey, L.L. *How the way we talk can change the way we work*. 2000: Jossey-Bass.

27. Baumeister, R.F., Bratslavsky, E., Finkenauer C. and Vohs, K.D. *Bad is stronger than good*. Review of General Psychology, 2001. 5(4): p. 323-370.

28. Keltner, D. *The Power Paradox: How we gain and lose influence*. 2017: Penguin.

29. Wigert, B. and Mann, A. *How Managers Can Excel by Really Coaching Their Employees*. Blog, Gallup News, 2017 [23 May 2017]. Available from: http://news.gallup.com/opinion/gallup/210989/managers-excel-really-coaching-employees.aspx.

30. Prime, J. and Salib, E.R. *The Secret to Inclusion in Australian Workplaces: Psychological Safety.* 2015: Catalyst. Available from: https://www.catalyst.org/system/files/the_secret_to_inclusion_in_australian_workplaces.pdf.

31. Morley, K.J. *Gender Balanced Leadership: An Executive Guide.* 2015, Melbourne.

32. Banaji, M.R. and Greenwald, A.G. *Blindspot: Hidden Biases of Good People.* 2013, New York: Delacorte Press.

33. Rudman, L.A. and Glick, P. *The Social Psychology of Gender.* 2008, New York: The Guilford Press.

34. Borrello, E. *Professor Nalini Joshi, mistaken for wait staff at functions, highlights gender bias in Australian science.* 2016 [30 Mar 2016]. Available from: http://www.abc.net.au/news/2016-03-30/women-scientists-highlight-gender-bias-in-australian-stem/7285312.

35. Simons, D.J. *The Monkey Business Illusion.* 2010. Available from: https://youtu.be/IGQmdoK_ZfY.

36. Edmondson, A.C. and Lei, Z. *Psychological Safety: The History, Renaissance, and Future of an Interpersonal Construct.* Annual Review of Organizational Psychology and Organizational Behavior, 2014. 1(1): p. 23-43.

37. Performance Consultants International. *The GROW Model.* 2014. Available from: https://www.performanceconsultants.com/grow-model.

38. Carr, R. *Coaching conversations.* Training Journal, 2008 (October): p. 64-67.

39. Brassard, C. and Stott, F. *Coaching Circles: True Support for Breakthroughs.* 2016: Impact Coaching Inc. Available from: www.coachingcircles.ca.

40. Weitzel, S.R. *Feedback that Works: How to Build and Deliver Your Message.* 2000, North Carolina: Center for Creative Leadership.

41. Goldsmith, M. *Feedforward: Coaching for Behavioral Change*. 2014: Thinkers50. Available from: https://youtu.be/BlVZiZob37I.

42. Heffernan, M. *Dare to Disagree*. TEDGlobal, 2012. Available from: https://youtu.be/PY_kd46RfVE.

43. Rock, D. *Learning about the Brain Changes Everything*. TEDxTokyo, 2013. Available from: https://youtu.be/uDIyxxayNig.

44. Unknown. *Planned Renegotiation: The Pinch Model*. The Pfeiffer Library Volume 26, 2nd Edition, 1998. Available from: https://korcos.wikispaces.com/file/view/Pinch+Crunch.pdf.

45. Amabile, T. *The Progress Principle*. TEDxAtlanta, 2011. Available from: https://youtu.be/XD6N8bsjOEE.

46. Groysberg, B., Lee, J., Price, J. and Cheng, J.Y. *The Leaders' Guide to Corporate Culture* Harvard Business Review, 2018. January-February: p. 44-52.

47. Morley, K.J. *How to Create a Sustainable Coaching Culture: Whitepaper#2 for Leaders who want to Create a Meaningful Legacy*. 2018. Available from: https://karenmorley.com.au/executive-coaching-whitepapers/.

Index

Acknowledgments

Lead like a Coach would not have been possible without the generosity and openness of the many people I've had the privilege to coach. Coaching you has given me a rich experience, which has shaped my own development as a coach, as well as given me the impetus to write this book. Thank you.

Being a part of the Thought Leaders Business School community motivated me to write this book. I would not have done it so well or so quickly without the intellectual elegance and rigour of the TLBS process. Special thanks to Kieran Flanagan for working through the title with me. It provided clarity and focus. That helped me to clarify my purpose for the book, and writing it then became a pleasure.

Big thank you to Peter for love, coffee and, importantly, help with those occasional, inevitable, technical crises.

I could not have had better support turning the manuscript into the final product than I've received from Lesley Williams and the team at Major Street Publishing. Thank you so much for your wise and efficient support.

Contact Karen Morley

Thank you for your interest in *Lead Like a Coach*, and for investing your valuable time to read it.

I sincerely hope that it has provided you with insight, tools and motivation to improve your leadership skills. I hope it has helped you to coach your people to be more productive, and that you feel uplifted by your leadership experience as coach. If you do, then the book has done its work.

I'd love to hear your stories about your leadership coaching journey, and I'd be delighted to answer any further questions that you have. Get in touch with me by email at kmorley@karenmorley.com.au.

Stay tuned for news about follow-up books! Don't hesitate to make a suggestion or recommendation about what you would like to read about – I'd love to write about the leadership challenges and insights that you'd like to know more about.

Please stay connected. If you've not already signed up for my newsletters and updates, please do so via my website at https://www.karenmorley.com.au, where you can also browse through past musings on all things leadership. You can also follow me on Linkedin (au.linkedin.com/in/karenmorley) or Twitter (@KarenMorley_KMA)

Finally, if you'd prefer the personal coaching touch, or to develop coaching skills in your leaders, then contact me on +61 438 215 391 or at kmorley@karenmorley.com.au.